Uncommon Sense
Children and School

DAVID M. WILLSON

UNCOMMON SENSE CHILDREN AND SCHOOL

Teachers, Paraprofessionals, Parents/
Caregivers, School Personnel, Service
Providers, School Leadership, and Others,
Understanding Roles and Working
Together Helping Children

2006

Uncommon Sense
Children and School

TABLE OF CONTENTS

Special notes will be italicized

Dear Readers,

Uncommon Sense books are being developed to offer readers insights and practical strategies to make their lives better in some way. Our authors may not be those with PhD's, or may not be people who have spent their lives in a specific skill area, but they very well could be. Uncommon Sense simply seeks those who are creative, say things differently, and, with or without specific education levels and years of experience, can help people.

This book offers you an insightful and practical exploration on a path to better the lives of children in schools. I am hopeful you will gain knowledge to a host of issues that can critically affect your ability to help your children realize their potential. The balance and teamwork between schools and homes has become increasingly unstable. Teachers, paraprofessionals, parents/caregivers, school leaders, and many others, working together as an effective team, present the best potential for children to be successful. Everyone must be able to accept both responsibility and accountability on the path to helping kids succeed.

I've worked with children and families for approximately 26 years in a variety of settings: residential treatment programs, schools, psychiatric centers, hospice, emergency shelters, and private practice. I have an associate's degree in human service technology, a master's degree in social work, a master's degree in counseling, and an educational specialist degree in school psychology. I have been a child care worker, mental health technician, hospice volunteer, therapist, special education director and school psychologist. The balance of knowledge gained through family life, personal life, work/career and formal education is priceless. It has been the integration of these experiences that have benefited my work with children, not one aspect more than another.

In this book, my experiences prompted me to choose areas I believe need to receive attention and be better understood. In the vast situational events and methodologies in helping children, my focal points are certainly not exhaustive, but I believe these areas have incredible significance to the social, behavioral and emotional needs of our children. Those who refuse or resist challenges that present in these areas seem to not understand the uncommon sense links between these issues and the child's overall performance in school. There will be some repetition in messages across the parent/caregivers and teacher, paraprofessional sections; I simply decided this was necessary. Throughout this book, use of the words "parents" and "caregivers" are often interchangeable. Paraprofessionals, and many others working with children in school, may also be considered interchangeable when the title of "teacher" is presented.

The challenge of this book is to explore issues that may be interfering with your development as a parent/caregiver, teacher/paraprofessional, leader, professional service provider, or support staff of children. If you experience some discomfort about an issue being presented, please explore your heart and mind and continue to read.

Sense! If Only It Were So Common.

Sincerely, David M. Willson, MSW, MS, Ed.S.
Uncommon Sense Unlimited

ACKNOWLEDGMENTS

I would like to thank the thousands of children who have crossed my personal and professional path over the years—children of all shapes, sizes, colors, and ethnicity. I would like to thank my teachers from formal educational settings, the workplace, and life in general, which includes parents, teachers, school staff and many others. It is from and with their help that I have found ways to work better with people—and learned ways *not* to work with people. I must thank an incredibly supportive family and friendship circle. To my parents, Bill and JoAnne, you are OK in my book and you've actually provided me the motivation and support to write one. Most importantly, I thank my late niece Jessica for the love and naive wisdom she offered during her life on this earth and the motivation she has given me to always do better work with children. I have learned things from all these people, really important things, and I continue to learn. I thank all who have been a part of my learning process.

I also thank the following organizations and folks, yet will ask forgiveness to some I may inadvertently exclude:

The late Bob Leonhardt and late Jim Thomas from the Friendship House Children's Center in Scranton, Pennsylvania. Also from my FHCC experience, JB Brombacher, Maria Cali, Bill Whitlock, Gwen Devendorf, Ernie Laskosky, Pete Tripodi, JoAnne Diskin, Maureen Veety and Dave Heisler; The Children's Home Inc. of Tampa, Florida. Also from my CHI experience, John Parsons, Marshall Schroeder, Larry French, Jim Hart, Steve Martus, and the late Jack McElroy; The Scranton State School for the Deaf in Scranton, PA (and Marge Marino); The Hillsborough Community College in Tampa, Florida (and Dr. Marilyn Lairsey and Ginny Zamora) and Donnell Gilchrist; The Hospice of Hillsborough; The Florida State University in Tallahassee, Florida and my professors from the College of Social Work and the College of Education (school psychology and counseling psychology programs); The Children's Home in Tallahassee; The following school districts that allowed me to serve their children, teachers and families: Leon County Schools, Tallahassee, FL (and Pat Keen); Wayne County Schools and the North Pocono School District in Northeastern, Pennsylvania; Washington Elementary SD in Phoenix, AZ; Bath County Public Schools in VA; The Kodiak Island Borough SD in Alaska; Ruby Salazar and Salazar Associates in Clark Summit, PA; The University of Arizona and the Arizona State School for the Deaf and the Blind in Tucson, AZ; and finally, The Child Care Association of Pennsylvania (CCAP), to which I developed my initial sense of professionalism in my work with children.

Some Key Points to Set the Stage:

*Parents/Caregivers: Become active in your school's Parent-Teacher Association!

*Teachers/Parapros: Become active in your school's Parent-Teacher Association!

*School/District Leadership and all School Personnel: Become active in your school's and district's Parent-Teacher Associations!

INVOLVE YOUR CHILDREN TO THE GREATEST EXTENT POSSIBLE

LAYING THE FOUNDATION

Uncommon sense" as a concept in my work with children is a result of years of experience with challenging situations involving children, parents/ caregivers, professionals, and all school personnel who are a part of children's lives. Though the concept seems simple enough, applying it to a situation may not be. People far too often say that an idea or strategy makes sense, or simply "is" common sense. In reality, the backbone of the problem lies in the probable misperception of the idea of "common sense". In fact, if such sense were so common we would not have many of the problems we face today, and specifically for our cause, with children and education. Hence, "common sense" seems often presented as a flawed argument. People apparently make this claim more as a method to reassure themselves they "get it", yet I believe most don't.

Uncommon sense involves work, especially at the front end of a problem, rather than the band-aid, quick fix solutions many seem to apply. Problems within the educational system frequently get reactionary solutions, but these solutions rarely address the long-term issues. For example: A school tries a quick fix (teamwork and commitment excluded) with a child exhibiting disciplinary problems in the second grade. By the time that child becomes a senior in high school most everyone in the school simply acknowledges that he or she has had problems since the second grade. It then becomes a moot point for the team to consider the probable ineffectiveness of the strategy employed in the second grade. However, it would not be ineffective to learn from such situations to help other children. The problems this child experienced may have been resolved with committed teamwork. Everyone working together could have spared years of teachers blaming parents, parents blaming teachers, the child's frustration with adults, and years of failing grades and failing social behaviors.

TEAMWORK AND PERSONAL ACCOUNTABILITY

I have observed over and over again where possible simple solutions to problems within the educational environment get met with conflict, denial, or outright refusal to consider change. I believe this is due to the challenge of change and the awesome responsibility of true teamwork — but, there is no substitute. All players involved must recognize what has already been tried has not worked.

When everyone is asked to do something, the change agent is not placed on one person, but the whole team. Many seem to want the "other" person to address the problem, possibly because of their own lack of faith in a positive outcome. Using uncommon sense is not about what cannot be done. **The approach is pro-active and is about what can be done.** It is about breaking down walls of belief that there are certain areas and issues that we cannot challenge or change. This book offers thoughts, ideas, questions, and starting points to break down these walls and begin prioritizing and meeting the needs of the child.

When working with children having problems, rules and strategies that include the words or concepts of *always, never, black,* and *white,* should be presented with good discussion. When they are implemented the team must be in full agreement. This is an incredibly important concept, especially when we are talking about consequences for specific behaviors (more on this later). I believe one should rarely say never and almost never say always. As for color as clarity descriptors, there are frequently gray areas that should be explored. This is a good thing. Gray challenges the team to work together, be creative, and meet the needs of the individual child. Please don't misunderstand, it is true that consistency of good rules and strategies are most often quite valuable, but when it is recognized that the child is not making progress something different must occur. So, the key issue here presents with the words "good rules and strategies". Consistent presentation of problems, be they in academic performance or behaviors, should clue the team that what is being done is not promoting progress. Most of us can recognize folks who will go to their graves investing and believing in one strategy, whether it works or not. The human ego is a necessary part of the human psyche, yet when the concepts of *always, never, black and white* mandate its existence, bad things can happen. However, adults who are truly working together for the betterment of the child increase the probability the child's experience will be positive. A team that purports being committed to this end, yet the child continues to struggle, more likely contains a weak link in the teamwork or the commitment of the team is in question.

My hope is "uncommon sense" will prevail and that this approach to helping our children is beneficial to you. Please be aware there are accountability issues all parties need to be aware of, but they are presented with no intent to offend. Should you feel defensive or offended, take a deep breath, maybe even set the book down for a bit and then come back to it. Please do not give up! You, and most importantly your children, are worth more than a defensive reaction that may block good things to come. You must genuinely confront what has bothered you in order to move forward. This book is not in the position to pass judgment upon anyone. If your defenses are that strong you are encouraged to recognize someone may have inappropriately and/or constantly judged you in your past and that your current feelings may be associated with that experience. Do you have memories of your past or do memories of your past have you? If you read on, this material could help you. The honest and direct communication that lies ahead of you is designed to benefit you in your role with children. I wish you the best of work because work, not luck, is the key factor.

*The overall quality and class of a teacher, school, or school district may be best measured by the manner in which the needs of children with difficult challenges are met. All children do not excel academically and need other avenues in which to develop their individual interests and talents. Please recognize the value of the arts, sports and vocational programs in schools. These programs have the potential to keep many of our children inspired in school. Children who struggle academically may find the positive energy necessary to sustain the academic fight because of the positive impact of a sport, art, or vocational interest. I believe we must also recognize all children who are academically successful do not necessarily function effectively socially or behaviorally in school. Sports, the arts and vocational programs can also affect these children just as positively as those who struggle academically. This general argument may have more relevance in inner city and rural/isolated areas where children may not see options that promote success for their futures. In such circumstances, these children may be more prone to depression and increased suicide risks. Again, the impact of sports, the arts, and vocational interests, may provide the outlets *and hope necessary to help these children survive through difficult periods and to then move forward. School and community leaders that consider these issues and address them are truly functioning with the best interests of children in their minds and hearts.*

GETTING STARTED:

I would like to prompt and also caution you on some possibilities as you move forward in your experience with this book:

1) This is your book and your comments may be worthy of protection as if it were your personal diary. If you cannot guarantee this protection for yourself, either write with the possibility in mind that another may read it or simply keep your words in thought.

2) This is not the time to make **you** look good to **yourself** or to others, nor is it the time to beat up on yourself. You obviously want to learn by seeking new/different information. Your honesty is an excellent first step.

3) This is also not the time to become defensive and place blame on all others, even if you believe blame is warranted upon others. It is a time to review and comment on your own issues/growth. We cannot control the growth of others, but you can lead and model by example. Please respect yourself enough to be the very best adult you can be for the betterment of the children in your care.

4) You are encouraged to ponder and/or respond to all questions even if you believe they do not pertain to you and your situation. An increased understanding of your own beliefs and thoughtful information processing can only add to your insight and knowledge.

5) Remember, you don't have to respond to the questions. Answering them does, however, increase the probability you will gain something from this experience. Maybe some areas you'll feel like responding and others not. In the end you will know if this material has affected or helped you in some way, shape, or form, whether you respond by writing or not.

It is important for parents, teachers, school personnel, leaders, and all other relevant participants to understand each other's roles and responsibilities. This level of understanding is a cornerstone of good teamwork. Therefore, I urge all parties make a commitment to read this book from beginning to end. What you read will not be all-inclusive for every type of challenge that may arise. Nonetheless, this material has the potential to give you a starting point to view things differently, if you acknowledge what has been done has not worked to a satisfactory degree. In your work with children, it will not be beneficial to incorporate new concepts and strategies if you do not garner team support; such support is integral for the child's benefit. Should you believe the ideas presented to be appropriate for you and your work with children, the identified team members, and the child, should almost always be involved. The development of expectations and consequences for behaviors identified as either positive or negative is a crucial moment in teamwork. You must specifically define what a successful outcome will be and how you wish to get there.

Now, just like the commercials/ads that tell people to not do this or that without a physician's blessing I'll say something similar. That qualifier is stated because someone is perceived as having a physical problem and they are considering using other physical means to address it. This is perceived as risky business because the human body is so complex and factors can be so individual with potential for harm without knowledgeable professional guidance. For our purposes, please remember there are adult and youth communication/ relationship issues that can be complex and further challenged by mental *health* issues or varying disabilities. These issues may manifest through the emotional, social, and/or academic development of children. Please recognize the need for professional knowledgeable consultation when developing a plan to address such challenges.

You are about to read material that challenges you to ponder the way you have addressed your specific concern/s and then to consider the need to make changes. How each of you choose to better your parenting, teaching, work and leadership with children and schools is ultimately a personal decision, yet when attempting to develop a plan that addresses a young person's significant needs, professional consultation is necessary. This, along with the strength of the team's decision-making, should remain consistent. Ultimately, there are no guarantees that can be made of the human condition, nor of the integrity of all team members, but we can lay a foundation that promotes the best possible outcomes for our children.

Please remember my earlier comments about the confidentiality of your book — the decision to respond in writing and response-discretion is under your control. You now have the opportunity to ponder or write what you wish to gain from reading this material. You will be provided space to comment prior to reading a topic area and afterwards.

UNCOMMON SENSE

SECTION I/ TEACHERS

Your philosophy on documentation:

_____

_____

_____

_____

_____

_____

_____

_____

_____

_____

_____

_____

_____

_____

DOCUMENTATION: WHO DOCUMENTS WHAT, WHY, WHEN, AND WHERE?

A good beginning point falls in the area of documentation. Keeping a record of activity that has evolved is a necessity. The litigious nature of humans in recent history, inappropriate care by individuals, and requirements of insurance companies prompt the need for good documentation under many circumstances. The handshake no longer holds its intended power. Nevertheless, documentation does not have to be an unpleasant experience. It is possible to develop a structured format for each event or meeting; include the reason for the meeting, the people invited, people present, date, time, particulars, and outcomes/agreements. Everyone attending the meeting should have had ample notice to attend, which should also be documented. Everyone in attendance should receive a copy of the meeting's documentation with statements of how and when the copy was delivered. Beyond the less than positive reasons for it, documentation has the power to hold teamwork and team members accountable for their attendance and participation.

Teachers or relevant school personnel should also document phone calls to caregivers and caregivers should document phone calls to teachers. This can be quite simple when all contacts are simply updates. The teacher marks the date contacted, if contact was made, the primary message and response. The caregiver can do the same. The same applies for brief meetings at the school when a problem or potential problem is discussed. It would be easy to say this is not always necessary, yet unfortunately it is safer to simply do it, especially since most of the focus will be on helping children who are having problems. If parties discussing the same issue have documented a meeting or conversation in different ways, it is necessary to have at least one other person of trust available to sit in.

If the school is attempting to schedule a meeting, please remember to invite both parents. The school office should have the legal/guardianship information you need. One should not assume that only one parent will attend and please don't assume this should always be the mother. Even if the parents are separated or divorced, both may legally need to be invited. The only parent that should not be invited is the one who the courts have determined unfit and/or to have no legal custodial role. Another reason may present if separated or divorced parents cannot behave together when at a school meeting. A decision must be made with such parents because the school does not have the time to hold separate meetings. Either they behave or the school support team may need to involve social services or seek legal counsel. Barring such a situation, the parents should be the one's making the decision about attending school meetings.

_____

_____

_____

Your philosophy on teaching:

_____

_____

_____

_____

_____

_____

_____

_____

_____

_____

_____

_____

_____

_____

PHILOSOPHY ON TEACHING

What a great job! Imagine the impact you can have upon the life of a child; and you will have it on every child in your class for every day you teach. It is very important to recognize this awesome power. Achieving curriculum goals is obviously incredibly important, but I believe attending to the "bigger picture" will make curriculum goal attainment for each child much more likely, fun, and motivating. Your challenge, since you made a commitment to read this material, is to consider much more than academics in your work with children. I am not suggesting you become a clinician; there are other professionals within the school to address issues from clinical perspectives. Regardless of any decisions you make, you will continue to have great impact upon the lives of children. I believe the questions you must process are as follows: Will the impact be in a positive way, a negative way, or will you even matter (which is a heck of an impact itself)?

I encourage you to recognize that depending upon the child's living/family situation, you may be the adult who spends the most time with the child. You may be the most consistent adult in the child's life offering compassion, limits, and role-modeling. You may not believe these are matters of your primary concern, but they are integral factors in a child's ability to learn, willingness to learn, and motivation to be successful. These issues cannot be separated from the teaching of your grade level curriculum. Hang in there with me. As you read, the necessity of this concept will unfold with increased clarity.

Let us assume grades are the cat's meow of the educational experience. Do you think you are the only one in the class dishing out the grades? Believe it or not, my friend, you are being graded by every child in that classroom every minute of every day and it happens every time a child says:

"I don't understand."
"I forgot my homework."
"May I get a drink?"
"May I go to the bathroom?"
"Samuel's bumping my desk."
"My Mommy said the homework was too hard."
"You can't make me!"
"I did a good job, didn't I?"
"Is this right?"
The list is infinite.

As a teacher, you are being graded when a child gives you a correct response, presents with good manners, helps a classmate, alerts you to a problem, and probably most importantly in a classroom setting, when they present an incorrect answer or inappropriate behavior. If you have a classroom size of 24, it is never just about the two eyes you are focused upon at the moment. There are 46 others watching and learning. If they are not watching with their eyes they are listening. Don't be fooled by lack of visual attention to you. How you respond to every aspect of verbal and non-verbal interaction matters. And here's a general tip to help build confidence and participation - whenever a child states they cannot do something, ask them instead to tell you what they can do.

What you are modeling will greatly affect how the children respond and develop within your classroom or school setting. This happens for approximately six hours a day (including bus time, approximately 7 hours), ten months a year. Let me repeat: This is an awesome power. Your children are going to learn from you one way or the other.

_____

_____

_____

_____

_____

_____

_____

_____

_____

_____

DAVID M. WILLSON

_____

_____

_____

_____

_____

_____

_____

_____

_____

_____

_____

_____

_____

Your thoughts on classroom management skills:

_____

_____

_____

_____

_____

_____

_____

_____

_____

_____

_____

_____

_____

_____

CLASSROOM MANAGEMENT SKILLS

I have said on many occasions that good classroom management skills are more important than one's level of expertise regarding the subject being taught. I'm making this statement on the assumption you have qualified to work in the classroom and/or to teach the material at least on an average level. However, without classroom management skills, how do you maintain attention, interest, motivation and cooperation from a large group of children? If you cannot, does it really matter how well you know the material? I'll take a teacher with strong classroom management skills and adequate curriculum knowledge as opposed to vice versa any day, especially these days.

It becomes a moot point to have excellent knowledge of subject areas if a teacher cannot provide a safe, calm, trusting, and consistent environment in which to teach. In order to give and receive instruction it is important to have an optimal environment. If the class is unruly or out of control, you might be able to get the material to a certain number of children, but this may be more a sign of those children's individual strengths than yours. Be honest with yourself here. Your skills in management matters. Think of it this way. You are an adult and if you are attempting to learn something new and the surroundings are loud, stressful or unpredictable, will you learn? Or think about similar kinds of conflicts you experienced as an adult when another adult was expected to secure/settle the environment or was expected to quiet the environment when being instructed/directed.

I remember three college male freshmen trying to bully another student for answers on a test when the professor left the room for a short time. I intervened and they attempted to bully me as well. The kicker was that they had problems when the professor was in the room. So I was thinking, what was she thinking! You may be able to recall disruptive talkers, arguers, gigglers, etc. What were your feelings? Remember, you are an adult. On the learning and developmental continuum most children don't yet have the coping skills to adapt or handle such situations.

I hear it inferred, and directly stated sometimes, that some teachers believe behavioral and emotional needs are secondary to academic needs. If this is an argument you are passionate about I ask you to consider a truthful self-assessment. I have often found this argument to be fueled more by a lack of confidence in one's ability to discipline than one of true philosophical conviction. I will argue this to my grave by stating these factors can almost never be mutually exclusive. Understanding and accepting your role as a complete classroom manager does not make the job harder, it should actually make your job easier and much more fun. In fact, your job should have a very significant degree of fun connected to it. If you are not having fun, smiling frequently, and simply enjoying the little, medium, and larger lives in your presence, something is not working for you. You can impart serious information, have serious goals, and maintain a very structured classroom setting and still have fun with children. As a matter of strong opinion, such a structured setting will likely allow for such outcomes to occur.

By design, children are not supposed to always be serious. They are suppose to find the silly in things, do a little teasing and giggle. Your job is to also help them recognize when and where it is appropriate to express these behaviors. Use their humor and your own sense of humor; it's a wonderful tool when used appropriately. You will no doubt have conflicts if you are not aware of this. Though you must understand the range of normalcy regarding age-group behaviors, the concept of the childhood spirit generally remains the same and this includes teens.

DAVID M. WILLSON

_____

_____

_____

_____

_____

_____

_____

_____

_____

_____

_____

_____

_____

_____

_____

_____

Your thoughts on discipline:

_____

_____

_____

_____

_____

_____

_____

_____

_____

_____

_____

_____

_____

_____

DISCIPLINE CONCERNS

Let me talk about the fear-based instructor. In his or her class, nobody "acts-up". On the surface other teachers may actually believe this teacher commands the respect of the children. A clear distinction must be recognized here. Fear-based and respect-based classroom instructors are two greatly different relational styles. The difference stems from their motivation. Fear, by definition, involves some aspect of perceived danger. Fear also appears to manifest when the danger is unknown. Children in school should not feel they are in danger and they should almost always know the consequences for there actions. The modeling occurring under fearful instruction is: "you will behave and learn in this class — or else". One can ask, or else what? I don't know what "or else" means either, and so the children are left to imagine. Being children, imagination is a primary area of strength. What can children imagine? —— Will she or he hit me? Will he or she fail me? If my parents have to come to the school, will he or she yell at or hit my parents? You and I know this won't happen (hopefully), but young children do not. To further defend such a teaching style some will say "whatever works". Too which I ask, what does "works" mean?

If the fear factor is a part of the teacher-child relationship, other teachers begin to pay a price. If this fear factor is happening in the home it will now be further reinforced. These children begin to accept that learning and self-control will only be possible when in fear of an authority figure. The wise teachers who understand the respect issue will be challenged, yet they'll pull through. However, the teachers who have limitations regarding behavioral management will be significantly affected when they are cross-teaching the identified child — and not in a good way. Did you ever see frenzied sharks searching for the source of a drop of blood? It's a frightening sight as are the results of cross-teaching relationships between teachers with poor classroom management skills and fear-based teachers. So, when I hear of a classroom that has serious behavioral management problems, I do not assume that the teacher is greatly deficient with management skills. I will also consider and assess the management practices of other teachers on the team.

I believe when a person feels they have to teach a class by instilling fear, something went wrong long before they arrived in the classroom. The potential now is that we have children who will obey out of fear. Many children with aggressive tendencies or bullying behaviors will find this style of teaching very reinforcing. Ouch! I don't know about you, but I want children to obey out of respect.

To understand the full impact of respect, you should first realize it is mutual. Most children will afford respect to the adult first, but there are some who seem to require the reverse. These are usually the children we see having behavioral (acting out) problems at school and it is usually caused by adults who previously injured the belief that children can trust and respect adults without question. Your goal should not involve a battle of "who-will-respect-who-first". Even the most difficult children will usually provide you opportunities to gain their respect before the situation dissolves into nasty confrontations. You simply may have blown the opportunities when they presented, or you never saw them in the first place. One thing to remember; respect does not have a fear factor attached to it. Respect involves good feelings; "to hold in esteem". We typically respect people who listen, who are fair, and who are consistent, even if it involves their disciplining of us.

Children who truly respect their teacher will cooperate because it is the right thing to do and they usually know the consequences for their behaviors, good or bad. This respect helps the child develop an internal sense of what is right and what is wrong, as opposed to the fear factor, which dictates a need for external control. If we are not nurturing and teaching internal controls, we are contributing, or at the very least, flirting with the creation of behaviors that the legal system may eventually have to deal with. One who requires external controls to do the right thing will eventually be without internal controls. What kinds of decisions will be made when this occurs?

Granted, most children vulnerable to such need for external controls are not vulnerable because of schooling issues. It is much more probable that parenting styles and/or clinical issues have been seeded. Regardless of etiology, school personnel do not need to be reinforcing the behavior problem. Please understand, there are teachers who are unfairly described as fear-based when in actuality they are respect-based. I've found on numerous occasions that some teachers, by virtue of their own limitations, will believe and/or say certain children only behave in certain classes because they are afraid of the teacher. A child might say they are afraid because the teacher is large, has a serious demeanor, maybe even has a mean look, and others may inappropriately capitalize on such statements. However, further exploration can sometimes clarify these situations. The student may simply respect this teacher and the verbal or non-verbal intimidation factor is not at all present. The child's previous experiences or hearsay may have interfered with their perception of the current teacher that stands before him or her.

I have seen teachers who had a good sense of this respect issue lose their heads and regress to fear strategies because they are simply human. Every now and then, even these teachers panic and try to inflict fear to regain control of a situation. The respect-based teacher will leave room for growth and eventually heal (attempt to repair the relationship) with the child because this kind of adult will not dig his or her heels in and fully blame the child; he or she will hold him or herself at least partially accountable. They will assess their own role and what they could have done and will do differently in the future. In these circumstances a few issues must be considered. Is the child so troubled they simply would not respond to a respectful relationship? Did the teacher simply fall into the trap of a child who has been conditioned to require or elicit such responses? This question actually supports the validity of inevitable outcomes for children exposed to adults who instill fear on an on-going basis. The fear-based teacher will most often dig their heels in and only blame the child. This reaction will pave the way for future similar reactions and outcomes, either with the same child or others, either within the same school year or school years to come. The unfortunate result is, at some point, bad things will happen. In this day and age, a teacher cannot move through a full career without significant problems resulting from such a teaching style.

_____

_____

_____

_____

_____

_____

_____

_____

_____

_____

_____

_____

_____

_____

DAVID M. WILLSON

Your thoughts on punishment:

PUNISHMENT CONCERNS

There seems a common inclination for many adults to rely on punishment to address behavior problems with children. This interests me because, again, uncommon sense must prevail. On a daily basis, teachers can confront and address numerous situations involving children and problems. You will burn yourself out if you consistently personalize. You may wonder why I say personalize. In my experiences I have found punitive approaches are most often invoked because the adult addressing the situation feels the child has personally slighted them by misbehaving or by not producing a desired result. This is a greedy response. The problems are not always about the confronting adult, but punitive strategies usually are.

As a matter of experience, significant misbehaviors a child presents are rarely about the adult at the school. It is possible an adult may do something (within awareness or not) that is a trigger for a child's misbehavior. However, a response that is inappropriate or an over-reaction is probable evidence there are other underlying issues. You cannot always know what fosters anger or motivates people to behave in certain ways. You can however, set limits with firmness and fairness while maintaining your professionalism and compassion for a child who obviously needs a different reaction other than angering another adult. For example, the child who always needs to go to the nurse, the child who appears to lie about everything, makes up stories, etc. Punitive strategies suggest you simply want these behaviors to cease. By taking that position you neglect or minimize the fact that the reasons for the behaviors are still a problem. Again, I'm not looking for deeper level clinical treatment here, but simple alternatives to punishment. Do children need to be held accountable for poor decisions? Certainly. Do schools need to have in-school and out-of-school suspensions and expulsions? I believe so. But such decisions and the messages given along with them should be well thought and done in concert with good team dialogue.

An alternative approach to punishment is one that considers the concept of logical consequences for all behaviors, be they pro-social or anti-social behaviors. I have observed children to react quite differently dependent on which term the adult uses or implies when attempting to discipline; "consequence" or "punishment". Children seem to associate a punishment more with something being given to them as opposed to something they deserved/earned. I did not say always because we know many children have said they deserved the punishment they received—at a later time/date of course.

However, when we are talking about a population of children who already have significant problems, something different occurs. Maybe it's because they have received so much attention for negative behaviors they've conditioned themselves to believe punishment is something adults simply get a kick out of. There are also those children so hateful of themselves they appear to thrive on being punished because it reinforces their low self-esteem. This is a terrible circumstance to witness and, unfortunately, is not uncommon. We can say these are typical oppositional behaviors, denial, or whatever, but they do occur. I have found placing emphasis on the word consequences greatly diminishes resistance to personal accountability; maybe not immediately, but certainly over consistent use and time.

The earning of consequences for all behaviors is a far healthier concept to teach children than punishment. Consequences for one's actions teaches internal control and internal control is a necessary foundation for personal responsibility and accountability. When we say to a child they have earned a consequence for a specific behavior, it is much different than saying I am punishing you for that behavior. This takes consistency and will-power on the adult's part because children who have been "punished" a lot struggle with the variation here. You have to keep saying, I'm not punishing you, *you earned* the consequence *for your* behavior/decision. This is a wonderful disciplinary tactic because its function is not merely one for future deterrence as punishment seems to imply. It addresses the problem at hand while fostering or developing that internal sense of control we wish all humans to have, and it builds upon a respectful relationship. Remember, the discussion about fear-based classroom management and respect-based classroom management? A child's perception of punishment can promote an outcome similar to ongoing fear-based respondents — I will control my behavior only when I fear someone or only when I will be punished by someone.

We know that punishment can be fair and we know that punishment can be earned. However, with a portion of the children who are identified as having acting-out behavior problems in school, the way in which you approach discipline and the words you choose when you discipline matter.

I hope you recognize the concepts I mention are not loaded with clinical skills. As a matter of fact, I almost always challenge clinical treatment issues being addressed within the school setting. I believe if a child's problems are to this degree the parents/caregivers should consider external help. The school may be the only place the child gets respite from whatever issues he or she is confronted with. When we do not assess this appropriately, we run the risk of prompting the child to view the school as a treatment setting. The issues are then brought to the forefront of the child's psyche and he or she may lose the ability to focus on academic and social development while in school. There are times when this may be appropriate based on the individual needs of a child, but again such decisions should be weighed very carefully.

_____

_____

_____

_____

_____

_____

_____

Your thoughts on bullying behaviors:

_____

_____

_____

_____

_____

_____

_____

_____

_____

_____

_____

_____

_____

_____

BULLYING BEHAVIORS

Please be on the lookout for bullying behaviors. I'm not talking about horseplay and harmless, playful teasing. The issue of bullying is what actually prompted me to begin saying "our children" as I worked within institutional settings. When I address such issues with parents, I often give the following message or one similar to it:

We protect your child from this as well. This is not just about the child who is bullied. If your child has this problem, he or she also needs help. This behavior affects good relationships with other kids. This behavior affects other children and therefore their families as well. It is important to understand we all have a stake in the well-being of each other's children. It is our business, because the behavior of one child in a school can significantly affect the lives of other children at school, for better or for worse. Take the allegation seriously and make a sincere effort to address the problem.

Also, please recognize a similar dialogue is sometimes necessary for teachers who believe the behavior of a child in **their** class is not the business of others. What about when classes mix, recess, assemblies, etc? If you believe in this argument with parents you must practice what is preached.

I will remain as supportive as possible and tell the parents I care about their child as well. I reinforce this concept by stating

I want their child to develop and sustain good friendships, but with these behaviors, that possibility is at risk. I have come to believe most people can tell when feedback is meant to harm them or to help them. I have been able to confront many difficult issues with parents and be successful because I believe they hear and feel truth behind my words. This may not occur in our initial interaction, but it usually unfolds with subsequent contact.

Bad things are going to happen if you don't address the problem. Ultimately, someone *will* address the problem whether or not you choose to help with a solution. The juvenile justice systems and jails are loaded with people who are/were perceived as bullies. The outcomes are likely to be much more positive if you and your school identifies and helps the bullies and the bullied. Children with bullying behaviors are worthy of just as much attention and help as those they bully — they're just easier to be angry at. The school must take control over the incidents of bullying. If not, other systems may eventually take over and address the needs of these children. If this occurs, you will in retrospect probably view the previous adults who minded their own business (maybe even yourself) in a greatly different way.

It is important to recognize that you put yourself in a disciplinary and authoritative role when you decided to work with children. You may not be comfortable with this, but you are placed there on a daily basis in your interactions with children of all school ages. If confident in your discipline skills, great! If not, send for assistance when something arises and develop your skills. You have to take some kind of action. When bad things result from such behaviors, there will inevitably be someone stating "so and so saw it and did nothing". You do not want to be "so and so". By the way, children with poor behaviors will find their way to you, especially the older ones. As they learn you have a limitation in this area, their internal green light will grow larger and brighter when in your presence. Take care of *your business* and learn how to address this aspect of your career. Only then can you move forward with confidence and peace.

Your thoughts on the quiet/withdrawn child:

_____

_____

_____

_____

_____

_____

_____

_____

_____

_____

_____

_____

_____

_____

THE QUIET/WITHDRAWN CHILD

This child is often a victim of their own behavior. It has been a challenge to foster a level of concern for these children similar to the concern most feel for the acting out children. Uncommon sense tells us loud and clear that these children may be experiencing a variety of problems. These children may be the recipients of bullying behaviors, may be suffering from some sort of abuse/trauma or they may be children with attention deficit disorder, inattentive type. Why then, do we have a more difficult time and even resist accounting for them? I think part of the problem lies in the sheer numbers of children in a classroom. These children are not as easy to spot. They may appear well-mannered because they are not creating any conflict. Their low grades may be explained, quite simply, by lower ability level, since they're never causing a problem and they appear to be listening or focused. I will say again, we know such problems exist in every school so we must be on the look-out for it. These children may be more vulnerable to very bad things than children who act out.

Internalizing pain and anger does terrible things to our bodies, minds and hearts and it goes on in our classrooms everyday. We don't like when a child acts out and we certainly don't want to see anyone hurt. How different then is the probability that there are children in our classrooms everyday beating themselves from within? The acting out child is sending noticeable cues they need help. The child who internalizes does not call out for help in the same way, but the call is being made.

I have found most teachers to be quite insightful when distinguishing between ranges of normalcy and more serious behaviors. "Shyness" is a good example. We are not talking about a child who is a "little shy" when the child appears to isolate from most or all interactions with peers and/or adults. Teachers are afforded the privilege of being around so many children that their perceptions of normal and abnormal ranges of behaviors usually become well-developed. I encourage you to trust your insights and feelings and bring your concerns to other appropriate school personnel (guidance counselor, social worker, psychologist, nurse) to help assess and address the situation.

_____

_____

_____

_____

_____

_____

_____

----

*Special Note

This in an appropriate time to address child abuse reporting issues. All school personnel have the obligation to protect children. Child abuse reporting laws are typically quite clear—when a case of suspected abuse presents, it is supposed to be reported to a designated agency. Every adult within the school system should become aware of the particulars of these laws. It may be that your school has a procedure in which identified personnel make the calls when such issues are reported. What happens if those identified to make the call to the child abuse hotline has a friendship with the identified child's family or the identified child's family has a lot of power in the community? The reporters are not to be the judges and jurors, provers or disprovers. Such issues do evolve. This is why the law remains clear—simply report it and let the appropriate persons do the investigation and/or allow them to make the decision to pursue the case or not. It is important for the person who initially expressed this concern to know the situation has been addressed appropriately. In the event a report is not made due to ambiguous reasons, all should know anyone can contact a child abuse reporting agency anonymously.

As for frivolous reports? They happen, as do reports based on harassment, and they are unfortunate. When such cases are identified, I hope the child abuse report agencies and the school leadership address each case appropriately. However, I believe most reported cases have at the very least some merit for the report. A good/strong family will be able to process a case that is truly not warranted. They may be defensive, yet they will eventually understand the particulars that brought the school personnel to make the report. It is possible that some caregivers will maintain their anger. Also, recognize that "unfounded" cases do not mean disproven, it simply means not proven. You simply have to remember you did the right thing in your sincere efforts to protect a child.

I will make note of these issues in the parent section as well. The primary issue for all to remember is that a reported case should never be about adults. It should always be about the child. You are there to help protect children and to also help your community's caregivers protect their children. Abusers come in all manners; relatives, friends/acquaintances and strangers. Your report could bring to bear that the caregivers were unaware. Be clear and confident in your understanding of this law, what your school's procedure is, and how you are reassured the report is made.

_____

_____

_____

_____

_____

_____

_____

_____

_____

_____

_____

_____

_____

_____

_____

_____

Your thoughts on racism (you may ponder other "isms" as well):

_____

_____

_____

_____

_____

_____

_____

_____

_____

_____

_____

_____

_____

RACISM CONCERNS

We should know that exposure is key for humans to understand and accept each other's differences. This is not just about races and color. We are so weird. A price is paid when such lessons go unlearned and these lessons go unlearned everyday. We appear for maybe some anthropologically defined reasons to resist and sometimes even despise difference and change. We have not recognized that this has little to do with color and race, and more to do with anything different/unfamiliar. Unfortunately, color is so visible and we've caused so much damage in the name of skin color for so long, it is taking a long time to let it go, heal and move forward as humans together.

A school would be remiss to believe that they have no issues of racism to be concerned with. Unfortunately, as long as there are any children of minority status in the school, there will likely be some form of racism. This does not mean outward nastiness occurs all the time. A strange phenomenon occurs when there are only a few minority children in a school and they happen to be well-liked. These minority children become the exception to the rule. People can afford to say these are "good ones" because they are not yet perceived as threatening their way of life. Watch what happens to the same community when the number of minority persons increase. Fear begins to set in and often without reason or provocation.

There are times when fear is appropriate, but we have to be clear of its origin. For example, let's say there is a 100% African American community and a Caucasian family moves in with drug dealing motives. The easy way out for a racist attitude would be to focus on the color. The color isn't going to jump off their face and hurt you, but their drugs, violence and weaponry that can come with it may.

For a school or school district that has not been exposed to a larger segment of a minority population, the probability for racist attitudes appears to significantly increase. The effects of non-exposure have created the illusion that the born and raised residents are the better humans and they can only be damaged should a minority population enter their utopia. But you know what? It has not been utopia. There have likely been prior feuds or problems in this town due to some people thinking and doing things differently. All things being equal, color included, we will find things different in each other. Some people will feel they are fortunate to be able to tag that "different" label on a group of people in order to gain some sort of power or status in the community. Read the Dr. Seusse story about the Star Belly Sneetches for a childhood lesson on this matter.

It's not about color; we've made it about color. Terrible decisions about color have been made for a very long time simply because it's an obvious difference. Understanding and accepting difference is a normal part of a healthy life. If you are not grasping this, simply observe children in groups. Watch how they pick, choose, and base decisions upon friendships, especially around the age of nine through sixteen or so. Developing children have developing egos and many, at times, will see differences as negative in other children in order to massage and develop their own egos. Most are not doing this because they are inherently cruel; they are simply trying to find their place. They are learning about relationships; differences, patience, compassion, and conflict resolution and adults are their models. If there are no adults muddying the waters with hurtful attitudes about our brothers and sisters of difference (this goes well beyond color), children will come through this without issues of racism or other "isms".

I frequently ask adults to explore their feelings about other races. What I often find are people either willing to alter their beliefs, people in denial (who have been noted to present comments/behaviors indicative of racism) or people simply refusing to change beliefs. I challenge you to ask yourself where you stand. My response to people who have these feelings in their hearts is this: I believe one loses their self-given right to condemn another human if they have in any way added to the problem he or she is condemning. So, if you live with these hurtful beliefs and you impart your beliefs to children, you should lose the right to complain or judge any other human being's behavior. I know an enforcement issue presents here, but if people consistently bring this viewpoint to the violator's attention maybe he or she will eventually "get it". Silence can bring good things, but in this situation it brings the perception of approval.

Sadly, it appears quite difficult for people who exhibit these behaviors to understand this life lesson, yet some do. I realize we cannot "make" people stop, but the more people not accepting of these behaviors, the more likely the change. Please know if you don't say anything when you hear such comments, you are tacitly approving. Hearts and minds are affected by non-acceptance in larger numbers. This does not mean to fight with people, just disagree with their comments. If they want to have a rational dialogue wonderful, if not, just move on. It's because of this behavior that this terrible issue is hanging around! It's kind of like non-voters. Don't complain about our political leaders if you did not take part in the decision-making process. You should lose that right by not using your right.

Some people appear to celebrate differences and not always with a joyous heart. We continue to acknowledge little of our similarities, of which there are far more, while our commonalities have the potential to take us to better places if we could see more of ourselves in each other. Most of us seem to give *a difference* the same power as one negative comment in a day of a thousand positives.

Special Note

The previous four areas discussed; bullying, withdrawn behaviors, punishment and racism/isms really challenge your ability to self-assess. You have to consider reviewing your teaching skills to see if you are in fact skilled enough to assist a child's challenges in these areas. If you became defensive during this section you have something you may choose to address for the betterment of you, your career, and most importantly the children you teach. They are worth your honest assessment and, if need be, your commitment to change. And, you are worth it. Remember, I don't want you beating yourself up about these issues, nor do I wish you to invalidate all the good teaching you have done. You are human and since being so, you are vulnerable to all the anger, mixed messages, and media portrayals handed down or bestowed upon you by your history in this world. You have the opportunity to change. You've always had the opportunity to change. Hopefully, your identified child's future will be the motivational force behind such change. If this occurs, please thank him or her at some point.

I also want to say something about the child who does not fall into the "social mainstream". Tragic events in schools suggest these are children in need of attention. They are typically easy to notice for a variety of reasons such as behaviors, clothing, and language. It is incredibly easy for teachers to simply acknowledge these children on a daily basis. Just say hello and don't expect or pressure for responses. The key is to let them know you recognize their presence. We have to connect with these children. We have to observe for abusive behaviors from "mainstream peers". Adults should never contribute to the tacit approval of non-acceptance of a child or of a specific group of children. You have to model acceptance to the children in your school. Bad things can and will likely happen when children not only feel persecuted by their peers, but adults as well. Trust me; it helps a lot when other children observe an adult connecting with a young person who has been designated by his or her peers as "weird".

Taunting and bullying behaviors are present and can be readily seen and heard by adults if they are watching and listening. We see, hear, and read of children being bullied or teased for their manner of dress and interests. These children may have much to offer if you intervene on their pathway to the fringes. There are horror stories out there about what can happen when our kids end up on the fringes. It is lonely and scary out there and it is a place you want no child to go. You do not want any regrets of inaction should bad things happen when a child ends up there.

If you believe you do not have the time to put much energy toward this I will challenge you to reconsider. I've observed people expending more energy to not attend to these problems. I don't believe you have to look hard; it sometimes goes on right in front of you. Be a good supervisor in whatever area of the school you are in. You are in a constant supervision role whenever you are around children in your school. This happens in our classrooms, cafeterias, hallways, restrooms, gyms, buses, and locker rooms everyday. Watch for it; hold children accountable for such behaviors. Learning responsibility and accountability can be a very good thing when done appropriately. Those being held responsible and accountable may become better people for it.

_____

_____

_____

_____

_____

_____

_____

_____

_____

_____

_____

_____

_____

_____

_____

_____

_____

_____

_____

_____

_____

_____

_____

_____

_____

_____

Your thoughts on physical contact with children in school:

_____

_____

_____

_____

_____

_____

_____

_____

_____

_____

_____

_____

_____

PHYSICAL CONTACT WITH CHILDREN

This is not usually a crisis area, but I wanted to share some thoughts about it. I think it's a shame that school personnel have to be so guarded against physical expressions of "like". I understand why for the most part; I just think it's a shame. I say "like" because I don't believe an *individualized* expression of love is typically appropriate in the school setting. Can you imagine a teacher, principal, or other support staff hugging and telling every child they love them? Even thinking about this recognizes the awkwardness of its presentation. Shoulder squeezes, pats on the back, shoulder, or head, or an appropriate hug do not have to signify deep love, but to a child they will most often know this means you really like them. I use the adjective deep because I believe most children can process the concept of love from a depth perspective if such a distinction is believed necessary. I can say I simply love children in a general sense and I have devoted my life to them because of this. Most children will automatically recognize that I like them very much, yet they know there's a difference in feelings between me and the love they feel for their parents and other close friends and family. If they are not able to recognize this then something else is going on and we can use such situations as teachable moments. There are situations when a vulnerable child may feel more loved by a teacher than his caregiver or family. If such a situation brings concern to school personnel, one would have to assess the reasons for such feelings. Fortunately, such situations are the exception, but all are worthy of attention.

I've had wonderful discussions when helping children (mostly pre-teens and teens) recognize the difference between really liking somebody and loving somebody. These discussions can be fun and challenging and ultimately very beneficial to the child. You don't want your child to easily love everyone as they do you. A child can place too much trust upon an adult who either does not return any level of affection (verbal or physical) or returns an inappropriate level of affection. In particular, this is a difficult concept for those little socialites in the school. Don't forget, you are or will be by virtue of time spent with them, a significant adult in their life and this is why an absolute no contact rule may be quite confusing and even hurtful at times for children at school.

It clarifies as the grade levels increase, yet the concept of healthy appropriate physical contact is important for teens as well. Pre-teens and teenagers are far more focused upon their physical presence and adults should be sensitive to this. Appropriate boundaries are a mandate and must be addressed when physically reinforcing a child or when a child is sharing physical reinforcement with you. These are opportunities to teach life lessons so you must know what to say and how to say it. I do not believe an absolute mandate barring all physical contact is appropriate because this lack of communicating is not real life. Should you observe this, it actually appears abnormal. I do understand, however, that very inappropriate adult behavior and allegations of misconduct from children have placed schools in this situation. I cannot tell you the best way to address this issue, but good judgment is a must.

If there is not an absolute mandate against physical contact you can express yourself in very appropriate ways and you can teach your children to express in appropriate ways as well. It's all about teaching and for high-need children this issue will evolve as important and meaningful.

In summary, it is the identified child that will need such reinforcement to help raise their esteem and motivate them to achieve at a higher level. The motives and manner of such reinforcement however, must be clearly understood by all on the team.

Your thoughts on children receiving or being considered for special education services:

_____

_____

_____

_____

_____

_____

_____

_____

_____

_____

_____

_____

SPECIAL EDUCATION CONCERNS

All that has been said to this point is now magnified ten fold for you, the parents or caregivers, and the child. Your role significantly increases when the problem either warrants a child's consideration of special education services or has qualified and is receiving them. This child may be exhibiting high needs in one or many areas. They may have a learning disability, a low level of cognitive ability, an emotional disturbance, a brain injury, speech and language deficits, or have one or more of a variety of clinical disorders (e.g. autism, attention deficit disorder) that prompt consideration and possible need for special education services. There are no rules about the mixture of these issues. Just as a child can have a learning disability and an attention deficit disorder, he or she can also be classified as functioning in the mental retardation range and also have an attention deficit disorder.

There is an infinite range of complex interactions that affect the basic functioning and development of humans. Weeding out such issues is no easy task and sometimes may not be fully possible due to communication problems the child may have. Nonetheless, the challenge of appropriate diagnostic information demands a higher level of investment from both the home and school district. The labels mentioned should only come after the best teamwork possible has not been able to meet the child's specific behavioral and/or academic needs, and the label has diagnostic credibility that will provide direction for intervention. A case-manager becomes the key to team communication.

Unfortunately, this population of children seems to be most vulnerable to the "blame game". Who is responsible for what? It really is a simple answer—we all are. The challenge becomes the specificity of, and accountability for, what each member of the team is expected to do. By simply being placed within special education should not automatically be perceived as better, nor should it be readily perceived as the best alternative. Without good rationale and teamwork, this placement can be a disaster. We now have a child who will be challenged by the label in which they qualified for such services. Though some would like to minimize this "labeling" issue, I cannot. It is not just how the child perceives the label, but how adults perceive labels as well. The key word here is "expectations". We lose control over the inherent beliefs the adults in the child's life now, or in the future, have regarding labels and expectations. Everyone on the team should be very clear on the expectations of the child. They have to be realistic, yet challenging to the child. The expectations cannot be decreased out of lack of faith and hope for significant success; and again, define success. With exceptional teamwork the child will quite often exceed expectations. I often tell parents and teachers there is no way to measure the child's heart. There is no way to initially guarantee what will motivate the child to move beyond adult-placed expectations. This is a beautiful process when it unfolds because it affirms the power of teamwork and the inner spirit of those involved, in particular, the child.

I would also like to make a comment about "Gifted Programming". I always want parents and teachers to understand the result of any label no matter how the label is perceived. I talk to parents about the *possible* repercussions of a "Gifted" label. How the child internalizes the label, how peers perceive the label and what adults do with the label. You can rest assured that perceptions will change from pre to post labeling. I encourage parents and teachers to observe for balance of social and academic achievement. I advocate all to recognize a child's need to experience fun, laughter and silliness. I try to help parents and teachers learn how to communicate a healthy balance to such a child. This child may need instructional enrichments to have academic challenges, yet social needs cannot go unmet and such needs are sometimes even "punished". For example, when reprimands and expressions of disappointment are placed upon the child for socializing prior to an exam and *only* a score of 90 percent is earned. Challenges may come from many directions for this child and even from extreme self-induced academic expectations. This child will likely need coping skill assistance when, and if, a peer says, "You think you're better than me, don't you?" or, "You're weird!" These comments can hurt just as much as the comments put out there to children with learning problems.

Don't kid yourself, labels are a big issue and we must be ready to help the child through such challenges. The self-esteem of a child is at great risk. Though it may have been low prior to identification, it can get lower. Please do not misunderstand me; I believe when a label is truly warranted and the team considers all angles, communicates well, and attends to the child's spirit, good things happen. Appropriate planning can raise the esteem of a child if true placement is necessary.

Educating them about their disability is crucial to help them re-establish a learning foundation. They can become stronger and the issue of negative peer and even adult perception is greatly minimized. Remember, the goal continues to be to educate the child to his or her fullest potential. In order to do so, the building blocks for self-confidence and esteem must be an integral part of this child's educational programming. Regardless, I would still like to see our educational system be either all special or all regular.

A special challenge arises when a child tested for the aforementioned services does not qualify to receive them. What happens then? The problems were significant enough to proceed with the evaluation process so they should be addressed regardless of qualification outcome. I believe a child should never be tested to simply answer the "Qualify or Not" question. I believe a child should be evaluated to determine how best to meet his or her needs regardless of the "Qualification" status. A good evaluation will almost always uncover causal rationales for the child's lack of progress regardless of qualification status. The child's emotional, social, and academic needs must be met whether in a special education classroom or regular education classroom. Much progress can be made in regular educational settings that develop good teamwork habits and that also promote good evaluations to guide them in their efforts.

The challenge is now to get the team (child included when appropriate) on the same page in order to address the problems from a different viewpoint. Simply by being tested, every child will not qualify for specialized instruction, yet the child should believe that something is going to change for the better. Qualification standards and evaluation procedures are often misunderstood or questioned, but it is what schools currently practice through state and federal guidelines. But, if qualification status is not your primary concern and helping the child regardless of the "qualify or not" outcome, then the outcome status loses its formerly attributed power.

Another important factor to acknowledge regards private evaluations. Private evaluations can be quite different from those conducted by the school district. A private evaluation may make a diagnosis of a learning problem and recommend special education services, yet the school's evaluation may disagree. Private evaluators are usually not privy to, or possibly not concerned with, state guidelines for special education identification criteria. For example, a child may have a learning disability on paper, yet his or her academic history suggests he or she has learned how to compensate for it. Learning may still challenge the child, yet specialized services are not deemed necessary.

There sometimes appears a belief that the school district is out to avoid special education placements based on a private practitioner's evaluation. This may be fueled by frustrated, angry parents or inappropriate advocacy, especially if the school believes such a placement is not warranted and the family does. On the other hand, a school's perception may be that the private practitioner is being rewarded quite well financially for their evaluation and they will continue testing until a problem is observed. The private practitioner or advocate may also not be aware of caregiver issues that have hampered the child's academic, social and emotional development. The school district may also say a learning problem of some sort may be found in most people with continued extensive testing, even

"A" and "B" grade performers. These children, however, have learned how to compensate for it. Children who are affected by significant learning disabilities for whatever reason have not been able to compensate for their deficit areas. Without good communication between the school and the private evaluator the private evaluation may not have considered the child's academic history, teacher feedback, or the state guidelines that warrant such a placement. A good private evaluation will include relevant school and family information.

This issue also has the potential to set up adversarial relationships between the home and school and again, it is often the result of poor communication. Ultimately, what may happen is the child being placed inappropriately in special education for factors that may have been addressed through regular education with "reasonable accommodations". With the child as the primary benefactor, the team should always specify and mandate such accommodations. Good communication between private and school evaluators will address the criteria for placement. The fact is both reports may provide excellent information. A team determined to help the child without *professional ego interruptus* will do just that—help the child.

Perhaps placement guidelines do need thoughtful reconsideration, but this will probably not occur if the diagnostic team (regular education personnel being teachers, principals and vice-principals; special education personnel being teachers, directors, supervisors; school psychologists and other professional evaluators; guidance counselors, school social workers, school nurses and parents) does not work together to reach a common good—a good based upon the needs of children. Together, school boards, professional associations and politicians can be educated about the practical needs of all students. Apart, we simply invite these people to become part of the "blame game" and this appears attractive to some because it redirects responsibility and accountability. Fighting the "good fight" takes courage and a willingness to take a hit. We will not always choose the best methods to help the child and the child will not always make acceptable progress. I'd rather take a hit with a great team as this assures the fight to continue, while the blamers argue/fight with whomever. A great team will reassess and begin moving forward with the child's best interests in mind again. Historically, all great teams have had this characteristic and they most likely became great because of it.

*Special Note

The issue of behavioral accountability for children with Individual Education Plans (IEPs) has reached many a conference table. I implore people to recognize all children must be accountable for their actions. In these cases, the team has to assure it had done everything stated in the IEP to help the child. If there were behavioral issues building, but not addressed in the IEP that could be a problem. If academic interventions in the IEP were not implemented appropriately that could be a problem. Regardless, an acting-out behavior of a child still must be addressed. For example, a child pushes a desk over because the teacher pushed the child with a reading disability to read in front of the class. The teacher not only needs to make amends appropriately, but the child should be required to pick the desk back up and apologize to the class for the disruption. The team may consider helping the child explain his/her frustrations to the class and the teacher may need help in explaining his/her role in this incident. These are sensitive areas and definitely require team involvement and decision-making.

In the event that a child hurts another child or adult, I almost always want the school and parent to consider suspension (in-school or out-of-school) and possible expulsion. The last thing the school, parents or caregivers should want to do is present the appearance that such behavior is tolerated because of the child's disability. Now, there are obvious needs here to be case-specific. Nonetheless, I believe the rules have been greatly manipulated through poor advocacy, lawyers not looking out for the best interests of children, parents not able to recognize the potential damage from lack of accountability, and schools not appropriately addressing the behavioral, social and emotional needs of children who have low-frustration tolerance.

An example that comes to mind is the child that has learned or perceives the school or teacher cannot discipline him/her. After an inappropriate behavior gets him sent to the office he is immediately sent back to the class. He boldly walks in and sarcastically smirks at the teacher, thus with all the nonverbal (sometimes verbal) power possible identifies himself as "untouchable and unaccountable". Ladies and gentlemen, I want all to know when the situation evolves to this degree the future of this child is at great risk. This is not a time to banter about what the school cannot do or how angry the parents are with the school or teacher. Do what is right and in the best interests of the child and clean up any other garbage afterwards.

When did it become inappropriate for an adult to apologize to a child openly (in front of a class)? When did it become inappropriate to hold all children accountable for their actions? When did it become inappropriate for a child to apologize to his/her classmates for inappropriate behaviors? Yes, we sometimes have to hold some children accountable in different ways, yet somehow the consequence must match the behavior. School Districts with skillful understanding of these issues, excellent communication with teachers and parents of all children, and exceptional Parent-Teacher Associations will address these concerns with integrity.

_____

_____

_____

_____

_____

_____

_____

_____

_____

_____

_____

_____

_____

Special Note

Children having problems need to see hope in the eyes of the adults that surround them. Children are incredibly perceptive to truth and hope. Be careful not to patronize them and caution yourself to insincere compliments. Only say things you truly feel and be careful not to say it too frequently where it loses its intended power. Please recognize the opposite; they are just as perceptive to despair and mistruths. What kind of power do you want to share with your child?

Do not be surprised if your child does not initially respond favorably to this positive message. The child may actually continue to pursue a conflict despite the positive energy. I have found several probable reasons for these reactions and they are not uncommon. First, he or she may simply believe it's a forced strategy to "get them to do better". Second, they may test the adults to see if they are sincere with their commitment to this new process. Or third, they may experience an increase in pressure toward academic, social, or behavioral expectations, which may in turn increase the child's anxiety level. You just have to continue. Be supportive, yet develop and/or maintain limits. Try not *to overreact to pessimistic comments from the child; at this stage they may truly believe they are not capable of positive change. Let them see your hope and renewed commitment to them. When the child perceives the positive energy as stronger than his/her negative energy good things are more apt to happen.*

_____

_____

_____

_____

_____

_____

_____

_____

_____

_____

_____

_____

_____

Your thoughts on the issue of grades or grading systems:

_____

_____

_____

_____

_____

_____

_____

_____

_____

_____

_____

_____

_____

_____

_____

GRADING CONCERNS

The grading of children in school presents varying challenges. Whether it is acknowledged or not, children learn differently, teachers teach differently and many teachers grade differently, not just on qualitative tasks, but quantitative as well. For example, the history exam with all true or false responses or multiple choice is graded easily, yet some teachers may give full value for misspelled correct responses while others may detract value for misspellings. Some teachers detract value for messy work while others don't. Consistency of grades/points given for homework assignments appears to nearly always have much variance. The possible result may be a child who receives an "A" from one teacher and a "C" from another. There will always be philosophical differences about the "right" way to grade a child's performance at school. I only intend for you to explore the challenges behind this issue.

I think you should be clear with the children in your class at the beginning of the school year regarding grading procedures. This clarity should also be shared with the parents. This would benefit you as the potential for defensive battles during the school year would likely decrease. Children having problems need such clarity. I believe clarity is good for all and the identified child is benefited so much more by less ambiguity. They are already experiencing confusion of some sort and more will only intensify the problem.

Another concern about grades falls into the area of teacher self-expectations. I've observed teachers to strive so hard to have their children earn good grades they seem to hold themselves accountable if the child receives low grades or fails. I will note this seems to occur more when special education placement has been ruled out. The teacher may then feel they are without assistance and may also believe a child's lack of progress will be blamed on them. I try to reinforce the teacher's efforts by citing other probable rationales such as varying cognitive abilities, varying motivation levels, and possibly varying parental levels of support. These and other factors have as much power to affect a child's performance as a teacher's skill level. Truthful self-assessment without undue self-criticism is always healthy and will help your professional growth. For your own sense of esteem, leave room for factors not within your direct control as possible success inhibitors for the identified child.

Grading children receiving special education services has other challenges. The grading and teaching demands are more individualized. This seems to be a difficult concept, or possibly better stated, a difficult concept for some to consider. Some children have to work incredibly hard to be successful at a lower grade level curriculum. The goal is always to increase performance to the highest level regardless of the child's specific issues. It is quite difficult to imagine failing children who are working to their highest capacity. By virtue of being in special education a student's age of graduation may be increased approximately three years. A very small percentage of these children should require such extensions. The potential outcome on self-esteem and potential age at graduation must be considered and these two factors are rarely, if ever, mutually exclusive.

Hopefully, this is perceived as an issue worthy of attention. My summary opinion regarding grades is as follows: The child who presents an incredible work ethic and receives consistent grades within the "C" range has great potential to be successful with his or her life due to such a work ethic. The child who receives consistent "A" range grades without such an ethic may actually have a tougher time in the "big picture". When a child is observed to work hard it would benefit the child greatly if you were to reinforce the work ethic as if it were an "A" grade, yet still be clear on what grade the child has earned. Consistent positive reinforcement of a good work ethic should be able to keep the child's esteem up even if not getting A's and B's. If lower or failing grades are occurring than the child's team should explore possible factors affecting this development. I believe this strategy is beneficial to most children. Grades do not define a child's future as certain, be they low or high. Yes, they are very important, but so to is the work ethic and inner spirit of the child behind the grade. How a team discusses this with an identified child is very important and is an issue that must receive attention. Good teamwork will find agreement in such a dialogue when developing a plan to assist the child.

Special Note

The issue of grades receives much attention when the child graduates from school and does not read well. Unfortunately, these situations garner much negative attention for the school from which the child graduated. I believe it is rare for a school to have simply passed a child along without attempting to assist the child's academic challenges.

The media, however, does not usually appear interested in reviewing what the school had done to help such a child be more successful. When negative attention for such matters is warranted I say go for it, however, be fair and have all the facts prior to making that judgment. Folks, the development of reading is not a given. It is like breathing—it comes so easy and automatic to most that it is taken for granted, but not for those with respiratory problems. The development of reading does not automatically happen for everyone. Learning disabilities and lower cognitive functioning can significantly impede this development. Special education services, tutoring and other interventions do not automatically result with reading skills commensurate to grade levels. We then may have children graduating who do not read well. This is simply not uncommon. Also, because of confidentiality and required ethical behavior of school systems, the school leadership cannot defend cases where the caregivers provided minimal, to no support, for the child in question.

When the school and parents/caregivers work together reasonable goals and expectations for the child should be developed—not reasonable goals and expectations of a news reporter or angry community member who know nothing about the child in question or the team's efforts in helping the child. What their argument infers is "make them read" or "keep them in school until they can read like us". This argument is inappropriate for obvious reasons. Attention to schools doing whatever they can to help children learn however is very appropriate. Helping these children develop their limitation areas to the best of their ability and building upon their strength areas is key for their future success.

_____

_____

_____

_____

_____

_____

_____

_____

_____

_____

_____

_____

_____

_____

_____

Please see Special Note re: clinical disorders and medication management issues in Section II: Parents.

Your thoughts on your relationships with professional peers:

_____

_____

_____

_____

_____

_____

_____

_____

_____

_____

_____

_____

PROFESSIONAL PEER RELATIONSHIPS

How do you want to be viewed by your peers? Does it matter? These are important questions for you to ask yourself. They are necessary for true self-assessment and it is nearly impossible that you learn nothing new about yourself during this process. Your beliefs and feelings about yourself and your work are intimately tied to your role as a teacher of children. I really hope you will be able to consider this concept as valid. The two questions I present are loaded with issues associated with your history in this world. For example, when someone says, "I don't care what others think about my teaching" there is cause to question several motivations for such a comment. Does this teacher believe he or she is surrounded by others who are all incorrect in their teaching styles or are all of lesser abilities? Is this teacher feeling defensive by someone's criticism? If so, was the criticism presented constructively or destructively? Is this teacher suffering from apathy? Apathy is a terrible mental health issue; the sufferers of it don't usually recognize they are suffering. Whatever the motivation, there is something that needs to be addressed in order to move forward.

I believe most people want to feel respected by their peers and maybe more so in professions that involve children. I believe there are few other areas in our lives that challenge the adult ego as much as issues associated with raising, caring for, and/or educating children. Most adults appear to believe the way they deal with children, in whatever capacity, is the "right" way. Teachers are no different. You are just as vulnerable to ego interference as the rest of the lot. Assessing your thoughts and feelings in this area is no easy task, but I know you're up to it. Should you recognize the desire for more peer respect you will have to develop a plan to gain that respect. Respect is earned. You first have to acknowledge why a lack of respect is being perceived. Finally, please recognize a perceived lack of respect may be your perception and you may be incorrect. It is always possible that those not giving you respect are the ones with issues in need of addressing. You may need a trusted friend, co-worker, or professional consult in this area in order to appropriately interpret your situation.

Some questions to ponder for your self-assessment:

Am I perceived as a teacher with low demands on children?

Am I perceived as a teacher with unrealistically high demands on children?

Am I perceived as difficult to get along with?

Am I perceived as lazy, doing the bare minimum to maintain my job?

Am I perceived as having a negative attitude?

Am I perceived as being a gossip?

Am I perceived as being a "weak" teacher?

Am I perceived as manipulative?

Am I perceived as always trying to align with people in power positions?

Am I perceived as not caring/prioritizing children?

I listed these questions because they are issues that do appear to foster either problems or respect for teachers depending upon the answers you attach to them. These questions easily transfer to other arenas as well. If you recognize yourself here, try to reinforce your first triumph — personal accountability. You will only be able to move forward when this occurs. If you find yourself defending why others may perceive you in such ways, you may have to request honest feedback from your peers. This can be quite difficult. Are you emotionally strong and mature enough for critical feedback? It would benefit you to only do so with people you trust and not those you believe would take advantage of an opportunity to hurt you.

Always consider surrounding yourself with positive people. People who are frequently negative about school leadership, teachers, parents, children, peers, etc. will drain you with their presence. The possible outcome of such relationships is that you will become them. You may not see this occurring because sometimes it happens slowly over time. Your closest friends will see it, your family will likely see and feel it and the children in your classes will as well. I believe negativity is like a disease. You have to consciously protect yourself from it. Also, if you find yourself constantly complaining about the complainers it's beginning to take hold.

You can express professional differences without being negative. It is seldom appropriate to consistently and continually blame a system for extreme negativity. We all know folks who do this. A system may have poor leadership and lend itself to critical assessment, yet it is people without solution-oriented resolve that sustains negativity. So, maintain your integrity and focus upon the children. If this is always your primary motivation, negativity cannot enter because when you do have something constructive to say, people will recognize your work and listen. If they are not listening to your message you must assess how you are sending it. More good news—positive attitudes and positive energy are also contagious!

It is important for you to explore to whom your primary allegiance belongs when working in the school setting. The importance of this issue evolves when friendships or politics between teachers, or other school personnel, become enmeshed with issues pertaining to the needs of children. If the adults involved are mature and/or professional enough to always place the child before the friendship or political motive, great! If not, the child suffers, and so does the integrity of the entire school and district. Decisions are then made that indicate the friendship or political motive is more important than doing the right thing for children. I challenge you to explore your professional self for allegiance issues or potential allegiance issues. Your children and your peers need this from you.

You can begin this process by understanding you are not responsible (this would be rare) for the inappropriate or unprofessional behavior of other adults in your school. Should a person make a poor decision that prompts them to come to you for support or cover, you should question the motive and/or value of the friendship. They are now putting you at risk to be questioned about your level of professionalism and integrity. A good person will not do this to you. They will be accountable for their own behaviors. Open and honest communication between friends and between professionals, and between friends who are also co-professionals, will decrease the possibility of such an event. Dedicated professionals and workers will demand integrity for themselves, fellow teachers, co-workers, the school, and the district in which they work. The worst possible situation involves repeat offenders. These people hurt us all through their impact on our children, our teamwork, and our reputations.

This book offers ways these folks can also grow as professionals, should one having such challenge decide they want to grow. When such a person makes a decision to not move forward, fellow workers have a responsibility. I've heard school personnel say parents will address such problems sooner or later through complaints to administrators. First of all, what if it's later? Secondly, what if it is an administrator?

I know the above situations well and have learned lessons from them. I've lost relationships with co-workers over such incidents and I've made decisions about employment over such incidents. I've learned such relationships lost were not worth maintaining for any price and that sometimes one must move on. I've learned it is not healthy to expect everyone will always like me. This acknowledgement comes with leadership roles, honesty, and professionalism. I've learned to assess myself when a work relationship sours and not assume it is always the other person's issue. And if the souring is of my doing, to then make amends. I've learned how important this issue is regarding my own sense of integrity, professionalism and personal growth. Though there were painful, stressful, and confusing times, the eventual outcomes were always for the better, personally and professionally.

As I near the end of my direct service in schools, I can

say I've learned how to address these issues more and more effectively. Perhaps most important to me, the integrity of my work with children, teachers, school personnel, and caregivers has remained intact and any argument suggesting otherwise could be readily dismissed through an articulate, well-defended and well-supported response. I wish this for you and hope this guidance will assist you should you be confronted with such an opportunity to learn.

Your thoughts on your relationships with parents:

_____

_____

_____

_____

_____

_____

_____

_____

_____

_____

_____

_____

_____

_____

RELATIONSHIPS WITH PARENTS

Most teachers do an excellent job acknowledging the power of good relationships with parents and caregivers. There are teachers, however, that do not provide the value necessary to the teacher-parent relationship when addressing such a child's needs. Some fall into the trap many parents do; one of perceived separateness (addressed in parent section). In essence, they state they are teaching the child, not the parents, and all other factors that evolve outside normal academic challenges are not their concern. So, I have to try to convince some that developing a different perspective in this area will be worth its weight in gold to their careers as teachers. We can then discuss what I consider to be very healthy/practical ways to go about such communication.

First, I will challenge you to always consider the possibility that the child you identify does not have "bad parents". They may just be parents in a "bad" situation. I believe you must move forward with this assumption to avoid damaging the relationship before you get to know them, and the situation, better. This family may be grieving, could be a broken family, could have a terminal or chronic illness within it, or be experiencing a variety of other factors. If such a situation arises, the school counselor or other relevant school personnel may intervene to assist the team with direction.

A sense that the school is out to judge parents in a negative manner will in no way help your teaching efforts with the child. You have to be strong here because these people may be quite vulnerable to decrease ties with the school due to sheer exhaustion. They may be tired of conflict and calls about the lack of progress with their child. They may view the time the child is at school as their time of respite. The needs of the child may be exhausting the caregivers. I recognize this does not present a good scenario, yet it does happen. They can be good people who are frustrated and tired. Your job is to consider this as a possibility. Patience and better teamwork will ultimately paint the true portrait.

I do believe it is the responsibility of the parents to sustain contact with the teacher/school. There are many ways a teacher can promote this. You can alternate phone contacts, use weekly or daily notes, or have consistent scheduled meetings. Whatever method is chosen, you have to be honest and direct with the parents regarding your availability for such interactions and the child must be aware of this communication. I tell parents that your teaching responsibilities do not allow for your role as initiator of all communication. You and I know a call will be made if a serious problem arises at the school, yet a long-term agreement leaves much probability that positive communication will occur as well. You also know that you must find a place/ time for positive messages in order to increase the teamwork necessary to help the child.

Behaviors, not words, will dictate the course of progress between home and school communication. When this is successful you will recognize it within the child. Don't be misled if the child does not respond favorably to such communication.

When a child is having problems they often seek weak links in the adult teamwork around them in order to maintain the status quo because change is hard. When adults align and the child cannot break the chain, negative behaviors can present because the child is being challenged. Consistency and teamwork most often wins, but it takes time. These problems are often developed over extended periods of time and it will take time to change them for the better. When I am involved in such a situation, I realistically look at grading periods as good times for assessment of progress. You are able to monitor grade performance, pro-social behaviors/skills, and attendance on most report cards. Decisions should be made by the child's team as to how you are going to assess for progress.

The unwelcomed outcome of poor relationships with parents or caregivers is an unwillingness to work with the school despite your good efforts and this happens, though it does not happen as frequently as some would believe. When the team is functioning well and the parents feel respected and productive, good things usually happen. If the parents are not working with the school/teacher because they don't feel respected or productive then you and the rest of the team must assess for the reasons and determine a next step. It takes a classy individual or team to be accountable for unsuccessful outcomes. In order to help the child this assessment team must "go at it again".

I've had many positive meetings addressing such issues with parents. Some sincerely believed the school was supposed to take care of all problems while the child was under their care. If a child is having significant problems such involvement is not optional. All of these issues are workable and changeable.

Something has to give; to continue on a course of separateness will most likely guarantee failure for the child across a spectrum of domains and academics is just one. Some people may get so frustrated, tired, or angry that the severing of ties with the school may seem an appealing option. Think it through—it would only seem appealing because they're angry, tired and frustrated.

Basic behavioral principles are at stake with teacher and parent communication, not only for the teacher and parent engaging in such communication, but more importantly for the child who should almost always be aware of such communication. Imagine, a child who truly suffers at school. Contacts between his or her teacher are frequently about an acting-out behavior, poor test grade, incomplete homework, lack of participation, etc. The child then has to deal with a potential conflict after the phone conversation ends. Imagine the possibilities if the child were to see his or her parent smiling on the phone and acknowledging a compliment made about the child. Imagine the results of a positive interaction after that phone conversation is completed. There is always a compliment available for a child, even if you have to look a little harder at times. The child's perception of school has to change and this is an integral part of that change.

If the parents are truly resistive to school involvement regarding the needs of their child, I sometimes suggest the school explore child abuse law; educational neglect. It may still be in there, yet not often used. If it is not, there may be a case for general neglect. I've utilized this law in a positive way on several occasions with good results. I believe the balance of home and school responsibility has been out of kilter for quite some time.

Believe it or not, many people believe communication with the school is optional. This becomes an even greater issue when a child experiencing significant problems is involved. This is not an option and when parents are made aware of this you'll usually see change. If change does not occur, enforcement of educational neglect may be explored. You don't want it to get to this point, but the possibility that it may should be explored and discussed with the team. These situations should help you appreciate parents and caregivers who are demanding and working just as hard as school personnel.

I want teachers to recognize the better their relationships with parents, the more likely parents will support teacher efforts. Such relationships also increase the probability the parents will reach out for help if significant problems are occurring within the family. For example, consider a family that becomes homeless and does not want the school to know due to what they may define as pride, embarrassment, etc. When these types of situations evolve, I would want the teacher to be able to direct the parents to the most appropriate resources. In the school setting this would most likely be the principal, vice principal, school counselor or school psychologist. The teacher with a positive relationship with the parent/s in this example may be the link necessary to get the child in their classroom the food, rest, and possible mental health attention necessary for the child to learn and be successful at school.

It is not typically a good idea, or appropriate, to fully depend on a child (age irrelevant) to relay adult messages, either by word or backpack. Decisions to do this must involve a team dialogue that accounts for all the specific variables related to the issue in question.

Special Note

Homework time is a crucial element to helping the identified child; home investment in this area is key. Problems in this area will inevitably sabotage the school's commitment to the child. School personnel can assist with developing a homework plan, yet the parents and caregivers ultimately are the ones to carry it out. A parent or caregiver must be certain and confident with their role and you must be clear about your expectations. Some parents may not admit problems in this area for fear of negative judgment. Be supportive and offer constructive feedback and guidance with clear expectation. This provides an excellent opportunity to further develop the home-school relationship. Even if the parents cannot assist with the actual homework, they can be guided toward presenting an optimal homework environment.

Your thoughts on teamwork and commitment:

_____

_____

_____

_____

_____

_____

_____

_____

_____

_____

_____

_____

_____

_____

TEAMWORK AND COMMITMENT

There is no substitute. There is little alternative. I guess it's possible to go without these factors in other areas of life, but certainly not when working with children having problems. I'll simplify it further and say not with children, period. Again, some parents, teachers, caregivers may believe they can "go it alone" or tell others to mind their own business when it comes to addressing a child's problems from a team perspective. The problems of one child have an impact upon other children who are connected in some way. A child will either bring friendship, joy, trust, compassion to those connected, or they will bring hostility, sadness, worry, fear, and mistrust. One way or another each child has an impact upon others. This is most important in the school setting because the classroom system functions on the team concept. Just as one child can energize a class by his or her wit, humor, pro-social skills, so can the child impact the class with disruption and fear.

I have recognized the need for these children to see a future that offers something better than their past. Schooling is about the future, while the draining survival mode only addresses present negative reactions to past bad experiences. It is easy to say we just want to make it through the day with certain children having significant problems. I implore you to recognize that the instillation of hope for a better future may be the most significant, meaningful, reinforcing, clinical, everyday-life-tool you have just waiting to be used. Yes, you may need guidance with this strategy, so seek it — from your team, supervisor, counselor, school nurse or whoever. Keep searching for whatever way such feedback and knowledge may come — just seek it.

I believe educating a higher need child is a great challenge which does not come easy; it's not supposed to. Good teachers will always challenge themselves and they will appropriately challenge the child. The broader assessment of a teacher and a school's character may be best measured by the level of success children with difficult challenges experience.

_____

_____

_____

_____

_____

_____

_____

_____

Your thoughts on renewing your commitment to be the best teacher you can be:

_____

_____

_____

_____

_____

_____

_____

_____

_____

_____

_____

_____

_____

BEGINNING OR RENEWING YOUR COMMITMENT

It would be beneficial for you to develop a system to write down one to three issues you wish to address concerning an identified child's current schooling challenges and be specific. Next, write down the first steps you want to take in each area to begin the process.

1) Issue:

Step I:

2) Issue:

Step I:

3) Issue:

Step I:

Now, identify your team members and make an appointment to discuss teamwork and role responsibilities. You may need support and guidance as you make your first attempt. You may want to consider having another school professional assist in the development and process of the meeting. These meetings are sometimes called Teacher Assistance Team meetings, Child

Study Team meetings, or Problem Solving meetings. And finally, mentally prepare to resist the urge to give up, especially when setbacks occur. Remember, this child's problems have most likely been around for a while and they're going to take a while to change for the better. One possible timeline to assess for progress is report card periods. Increases in grades, prosocial skills/behaviors and attendance are usually well tracked on elementary school report cards. For middle and high school age children, the social and behavioral issues may have to be assessed through other means. For obvious reasons, physical safety issues must be met with immediate interventions.

Following are concepts and strategies to **consider** while you either prepare your presentation to your team or while your informal team discusses the case. This is only an example; your school/system may already have a process in place.

1) Acknowledge that what has been done to help the child is not currently working. Share your concerns with the team and what you would like the child to accomplish—be practical and realistic.

2) An open-minded assessment of your abilities and strategies used with the child should be conducted.

3) Identify (no action at this point, just identify) all appropriate team members such as: Parents or caregivers; nurse and physician if medical issues are involved (for example medication management and monitoring); professionals outside of the school such as therapists, etc.; school/guidance counselor, vice principal and/or principal, and other relevant

professionals within the school. This list is not exhaustive. There may be other significant family members involved in the life of the child that should be considered.

4) Discuss the process of setting up a formal meeting. One should not assume the child's caregivers can read, write, sustain attention, etc. A call by the appropriate school professional could be made that gently explores these issues prior to the meeting. This information is critical in garnering caregiver support and understanding for the child and could also prevent embarrassing moments at the meeting. If there are any known or stated physical disabilities the school liaison must ask if any accommodations are necessary. When these messages are relayed with professionalism and compassion a caregiver is more likely to share any such challenges. At the very least it opens the door to communicate about such issues, if not at the first meeting maybe in a future meeting or discussion.

5) Your school may already have something in place as this may be the beginning of your Child Study or Problem Solving team model. Too many people in a first meeting can be overwhelming and even intimidating to parents or others. Pre-determine who will take the lead communication role for the child in the school's behalf and who is to document the events and plan resulting from the meeting. Commit to a new plan of action and establish timelines and team member roles and responsibilities. The

lead communicator must be a person with good interpersonal skills as the school's sincerity in helping the child must come across to the caregivers. It is good practice to be teaching all teachers to lead such conferences.

The primary caregivers should have a central placement at the conference. They are the primary recipients of the information the teachers have to share. A central seating location accounts for this and also presents as respecting the information they may have to share. The dynamics of the seating arrangement should be thought through and discussed prior to the meeting.

Please keep in mind that prior to such a meeting taking place many less formal strategies to assist the child should have occurred between teachers and caregivers.

_____

_____

_____

_____

_____

_____

_____

_____

A Few Summary Points

Again, this material is not intended to include all possible problems you may encounter in your teaching of children. Your passion to teach will afford you new information and the opportunity to explore and experiment with new strategies everyday.

It is also time to recognize that children's needs, regardless of severity, should no longer be viewed as automatically moving toward the path of special education. The "Response to Intervention" model (also known as the Problem Solving Model) is designed to assist children with significant learning challenges in regular education through teamwork across professional disciplines within the school setting. This model can merge special and regular education the way it may prove most useful and successful for children. Should this movement take hold across our public school systems, the percentage of children receiving special education labels and services should significantly decrease. Special education labels would no longer be required to assist children with intensive needs. Short-term intensive services may be implemented and last through a school year. Such an intervention could be provided with teamwork from **all** teachers and other service providers. This model has the potential to truly protect children from unnecessary and/or inappropriate placements. The primary goal of such a system is to help children bring their academic (reading most frequently) levels up to, or near, their same grade level peers. This would be an intensive intervention and time well spent if the child's academic struggles are resolved and they can move forward with more typical academic instruction and pace.

In the case where significant progress is not indicated the validity and appropriateness of special education services may be determined to be in the best interests of the child. It will be wise for you to begin educating yourself about these systems, though not new in concept, they are gaining ground across the nation.

_____

_____

_____

_____

_____

All that being said,

WELCOME

TO

THE

GOOD FIGHT!

UNCOMMON SENSE

SECTION II/ PARENTS

PARENTS AND CAREGIVERS,

Through this section, I am hopeful you will gain new insights and strategies to address a host of issues. Issues that can critically affect your ability to help your children realize their potential, particularly if they experience problems at school. The balance and teamwork between schools and homes has become increasingly unstable. It is time for teachers, caregivers, school leaders, school personnel, and others to work together as an effective team. Everyone is expected to accept both responsibility and accountability on the path to helping kids succeed.

Sense! If Only It Were So Common.

Sincerely,
David M. Willson, MSW, MS, Ed.S.
Uncommon Sense Unlimited

Please remember my earlier comments about the confidentiality of your book — the decision to respond in writing and response-discretion is under your control. You now have the opportunity to ponder or write what you wish to gain from reading this material. You will be provided space to comment prior to reading a topic area and afterwards.

Your thoughts on documentation:

_____

_____

_____

_____

_____

_____

_____

_____

_____

_____

_____

_____

_____

_____

DOCUMENTATION: WHO DOCUMENTS WHAT, WHY, WHEN, AND WHERE?

A good beginning point falls in the area of documentation. Keeping a record of activity that has evolved is a necessity. The litigious nature of humans in recent history, inappropriate care by individuals, and requirements of insurance companies prompt the need for good documentation under many circumstances. The handshake no longer holds its intended power. Nevertheless, documentation does not have to be an unpleasant experience. It is possible to develop a structured format for each event or meeting; include the reason for the meeting, the people invited, people present, date, time, particulars, and outcomes/agreements. Everyone attending the meeting should have had ample notice to attend, which should also be documented. Everyone in attendance should receive a copy of the meeting's documentation with statements of how and when the copy was delivered. Beyond the less than positive reasons for it, documentation has the power to hold teamwork and team members accountable for their attendance and participation.

Teachers or relevant school personnel should also document phone calls to caregivers and caregivers should document phone calls to teachers. This can be quite simple when all contacts are simply updates. The teacher marks the date contacted, if contact was made, the primary message and response. The caregiver can do the same. The same applies for brief meetings at the school when a problem or potential problem is discussed. It would be easy to say this is not always necessary, yet unfortunately it is safer to simply do it, especially since most of the focus will be on helping children who are having problems. If parties discussing the same issue have documented a meeting or conversation in different ways, it is necessary to have at least one other person of trust available to sit in.

If the school is attempting to schedule a meeting, please remember to invite both parents. The school office should have the legal/guardianship information you need. One should not assume that only one parent will attend and please don't assume this should always be the mother. Even if the parents are separated or divorced, both may legally need to be invited. The only parent that should not be invited is the one who the courts have determined unfit and/or to have no legal custodial role. Another reason may present if separated or divorced parents cannot behave together when at a school meeting. A decision must be made with such parents because the school does not have the time to hold separate meetings. Either they behave or the school support team may need to involve social services or seek legal counsel. Barring such a situation, the parents should be the one's making the decision about attending school meetings.

Parents and Caregivers,

Your cooperation and understanding in this area is crucial. Please do everything possible to work through difficult relationship and legal issues in order to communicate effectively with the school. This is in the best interests of your child or children.

Your thoughts on the role of intact biological parents and the schooling of their child:

_____

_____

_____

_____

_____

_____

_____

_____

_____

_____

_____

_____

_____

BIOLOGICAL PARENTS

Children having problems in school need the team's full attention — and that includes both parents. The one-parent-school-responsibility theory is possible when a child is not having problems at school. Nonetheless, the involvement of both will increase the probability for better emotional, social and academic outcomes for most children. I can say with much certainty, however, a child having academic, social or behavioral problems will not likely see significant progress without involving both parents as supportive parts of the problem solving team. This is where "uncommon sense" prevails again. You both brought this child into the world and you are both significant in the child's life.

This child needs you both, especially when times get rough. It is important to acknowledge issues going on within the family that may be challenging the child's progress at school. If there are, yet one parent feels they are not significant in the child's life and that the other parent can handle the problem, we have "uni-parenting" by default or somebody's fault. This practice will greatly challenge the well-being of your child. This is not healthy. This uni-parenting appears to cease working when the problem gets ahead of you and the problem usually gets ahead of you when this practice is assumed and/or employed.

If there are problems in the marital relationship, such as poor communication between spouses, parenting issues, alcoholism, substance abuse, or chronic illness (to name only a few) you must recognize these are not the school's fault, nor are financial problems — "We both have to work and don't have time to be involved with the school", or "We can't afford time off to go to the school". You'll have to do your very best to work this out because financial problems can change for the better over time. Problems with your child won't necessarily change for the better and without being addressed will most certainly get worse. Academic, emotional, social, and behavioral functioning often takes hits for such family problems. Good school personnel should be able to work with you to help your child be successful in school.

Parents having problems within their marriage seem prone to blame teachers and school personnel for a child's problems in school. It may seem easier to go this route rather than address the marital discord, but it will increase the intensity of the schooling problems for the child and it will lengthen the duration of the schooling problems for the child. While there may be school personnel that have the ability to pull the worst out of a child, the way in which a child expresses their frustration or anger is a reflection of the coping skills developed in the home.

If there is a family problem, it is important to accept your responsibilities and short comings and don't look for scapegoats. More often than not, school personnel will be aware of external problems, maybe not the specific details of them, but they'll be aware. The important thing is to get the help you need to address family issues and align with the school for teamwork and support in order to help your child. Doing so will greatly increase the probability for positive outcomes.

_____

_____

_____

_____

_____

_____

_____

_____

_____

_____

_____

_____

_____

_____

Your thoughts on the role of single parents and the schooling of their child:

_____

_____

_____

_____

_____

_____

_____

_____

_____

_____

_____

_____

_____

SINGLE PARENTS: SEPARATED, DIVORCED, DECEASED SPOUSE, NEVER MARRIED

I have worked with some incredible single parents who are on a mission to raise their children in spite of adversities that have challenged them. When problems arise with a child in such a family it is important to emphasize that single parenthood is not the school's fault. On the other hand, the school can become somewhat of an extended family so it is important to work with and not alienate the school if your child is having problems. Good school personnel will recognize your efforts and challenges and work with you.

It is important to acknowledge the circumstances surrounding your singledom. The different reasons people become single parents are significant and present many serious challenges to teamwork. First, how does the single parent's relationships affect the child? If you, as parents, are separated or divorced, how have you handled the separation or divorce? Have you prioritized the child's needs or is it a bitter situation where one or both of you use the child as a weapon against the other? The latter presents young children that may be unaware of a parent's negative manipulative behaviors, but at some point in time, in one way or another, the child will become aware and address such behaviors in his or her own way. Prioritizing the needs of your child or children is always the better option.

Divorce and separation are situations that call for uncommon sense. I strongly suggest you maintain your integrity and dignity for the benefit of the child. If you can do so, you may not see immediate rewards in the short-term; however, your child will never forget that you did not demean the other parent (in front of them), nor did you ever use them to express your anger against the other parent. In the bigger picture you will model incredible coping skills that involve lessons of love, compassion, priority, restraint, conflict resolution and possibly some others as well.

Many children have told me how angry they are with the parent who engages or engaged in such behavior, yet they do not express this to the identified parent. Often the anger is expressed at the parent who does not engage in these inappropriate actions. On the surface this may not be acknowledged by either parent and possibly not the child either. This reaction is not uncommon. Think about how the angry parent expresses him or herself in front of the child. I suspect the child does not want to be the recipient of such anger. It is safer to express anger and frustration around people you trust and people you know won't reject you, so the child vents on the more appropriate parent — the one with better coping skills and a higher level of emotional maturity. I wouldn't carve this theory in stone, but it does appear to present quite frequently.

One way I deal with this is through attempts to engage both parents. Whether or not both choose to be involved in the child's education is a decision they are ultimately accountable for. It is important to make the attempt to include both in the problem solving process. I communicate with both parents that the overall success of the child is dependent on the best of teamwork.

When I discuss this with parents, I usually make the following plea, "If you love your son or daughter more than you do the anger you have toward each other, your child has a great chance of overcoming their problems. Which of you does not want to help your child? It is through your actions, not just words, that will help resolve the problems and better the life of your child".

It is important to remember that the *reasons* for your separation and/or divorce are *not your child's problem*. If you blame this on your child in any way, shape or form, it is vital you re-examine the situation. The fact that a divorce or separation has happened, however, *is usually a problem for a child*. From their perspective, regardless of how old they are, you both have been with them their entire life. This again, is uncommon sense. Time is relative. For example, if the child is 6 years old, those 6 years is his or her entire lifetime. From the child's perspective you both have been with him or her forever. These 6 years of forever may not seem like forever to you, but you should not be thinking about you in this situation. You must re-examine the situation and remember a child should never be blamed for having the power to disrupt the lives of two adults who *love each other* and are *committed to team parenting*. So, if blame upon the child has evolved, guess what may be in question?

There are certainly situations and conditions in life that can take even the best of parents to task, like raising a child with special physical, mental or medical needs. I have seen this happen and I have seen such parents be greatly challenged as a couple, yet I have not seen the child blamed by emotionally mature adults under these circumstances. If a breakdown in marital status occurs it may be more a sign of poor communication and/or lack of investment in seeking appropriate human resources.

The bottom line is children should not be used to resolve parental problems and they cannot be used as weapons in the parents' struggle against each other. In reality however, children are used as weapons, effective pawns if you will, especially *if a parent's or both parents' love for the child is weaker than the negative feelings they have toward the other or each other.* If this is the case, I would like you to actually say that out loud to yourself. If you can make that statement without anything very strange happening within you, then you should probably seek assistance immediately. I am not saying this to be hurtful, but I am quite sincere when I say if you are that angry you really do need help. That level of anger usually does not dissipate by itself. You need to acknowledge this to yourself in order to better your life and to also cease hurting others.

When parents are having difficulty with these issues I usually find some mutual accountability. It is rare that one party is totally responsible for such problems. It is vital to remember that the child still loves both parents, no matter how difficult an angry parent or parents may be. Most people recognize in some instances a child may actually be better off with minimal contact from a very troubled parent. But you can't be the one to make that decision. You can pursue it through legal means, but there has to be checks and balances for such situations otherwise every angry divorced parent would at least consider attempting to sever the ties between the other parent and their children.

If you react in a way to damage that love, you will confuse the child and most likely damage your relationship with him or her in return. If you are sneaky about it, you may believe very small, infrequent slights will not hurt the child. In fact, these behaviors may seem (at the moment) to *benefit you* by *allowing you* to vent *your* anger, but this at the expense of your child. Your child, with great likelihood, will remember this. You probably won't be given notice when he or she may be ready or compelled to bring up the issue, but you will still probably react like it's coming from "out of the blue". Allow me to clear this up for you so you don't have to be confused by the "blue". There's almost always a rationale for human behavior and in such a case as this, you can be pretty sure your past behaviors played a significant role in the angry adult (passive or active aggression) you will see before you or, don't see before you because his or her personal choice may be to not have you in their life.

The child may not remember a lot of the manipulative, inappropriate behaviors the troubled caregiver/s bestowed upon them on a conscious level. Inappropriate, manipulative, hurtful behaviors and comments can be remembered through psychological means and may end up manifesting in the behaviors of your son or daughter and in future relationships. Do you want this outcome for your child? I really want you to hear this, especially if you are venting about teachers not helping or even damaging your child. You are their most important teachers! Are you teaching lessons you want to be taught. Trust me; they are learning from you no matter which way you decide to handle your conflicts. Children who are able to learn from their parent's mistakes are not as common as children who simply learn from their parents—for the better or worse.

I'm sure by now you have experienced some feelings. Learn from your feelings. Did you react to something I said because you have experience in the matter? Good, you are supposed to have feelings when someone or something addresses these very serious issues. Now, do something positive about it. Explore your level of responsibility; explore what you can do differently to make your life and your child's life better. You do not have to love or have great admiration for the other parent, but you should be able to acknowledge how important they may be to your child's overall development.

I'm hoping you don't come up blank here because there is always something that can be done differently. Go ahead and give yourself some credit. You can come up with some good ideas.

_____

_____

_____

_____

_____

_____

_____

_____

Special Note:

The factors surrounding your life as a single parent (by choice or not) can be incredibly varied. I can only say be aware of the possible impact upon your child. I must also acknowledge that being a single parent may not be a bad thing in the case of problematic relationships. Never marrying or possibly not knowing who the other biological parent is happens sometimes, and many such families survive and do well. Be aware that at some point your child or children will ask questions. It is healthy for children to ask these questions. Loving, safe, and honest communication sets the groundwork for a child's belief that his or her questions are OK and important. Do you think they do not notice something is different within their family? If they don't ask questions as they get older I would ponder why. Do all you can do to help your child and, should problems arise in school, have a plan to address them with the school personnel.

* Please read the special note in the teacher section on child abuse reporting laws. It will benefit you to understand school procedures should you experience this. It will also benefit you to understand the sincere motives of school personnel when such reports must be made. As for frivolous and/or harassment motivated reports, they are very infrequent and should be dealt with appropriately through legal counsel.

Your thoughts on the school's role with a grieving child/family:

_____

_____

_____

_____

_____

_____

_____

_____

_____

_____

_____

_____

_____

GRIEF WITHIN THE FAMILY

Issues surrounding the death of a parent, sibling, relative, or close family friend must also be understood in the context of the child's schooling. You must be able to recognize how such a loss is impacting upon your child. If *you* are struggling and do not have a support system, or refuse to seek support, you must know your child or children are also struggling. Please do not misinterpret a child's lack of visual and/or verbal presentation of suffering. I have found children will often attempt to protect the surviving parent when they see their parent is not coping well with the loss. The child, in turn, becomes the little adult.

Children do not have the coping skills in place yet to deal with such a tragedy. You are the one that is supposed to help teach this life lesson. At the same time of your suffering, children still need you to be the parent and address all the basic needs they have. You are human and it is OK for the child to see your pain. In fact, it is healthy to share this together. Yet there is no easy way around it, you are the one who needs to reassure the child you will all survive the loss. If you cannot do this, you must consider external supports such as family, friends and/or professional assistance. If you are not presently able to meet this challenge it may mean you have not allowed your support systems to help. The school can also play a very supportive role. School professionals can help monitor the child's reaction through the grieving process. A child's grief may show itself in changes in grades. Some children's grades will drop, while others may actually increase. The child may react to situations with anger, sadness, or with an appearance of calm. There are no rules. It is normal to see a decrease in performance and it is not abnormal to see a child invest him or herself more in school as a coping skill.

There are many facets of grief that most people can understand and there are well researched theories about grief that are helpful. There are universal commonalities in how people grieve; however, if you have experienced grief yourself you know that the experience is also highly individual. Your experience with grieving and loss is *your* experience and that cannot be duplicated or fully understood by others. What is normal becomes irrelevant and the subjective experience dominates. For those who have not experienced such a loss, their objectivity has a purpose. It can assist in the process of maintaining or creating some semblance of normalcy and consistency for your child and is often better achieved without intense emotions clouding judgment. We still want this to be attained with patience and compassion.

The team can help monitor the so called "normalcy" of the grieving process. This is important because a responsible group of adults can help protect and intervene should a child begin to self-destruct socially, behaviorally, or academically. This group of adults should be able to differentiate between healthy and unhealthy expressions of grief. If they cannot, the responsible group of adults should seek professional consult. In short, communication with school personnel is vital to monitor the progress of your child's grieving process and its impact upon the child's emotional, social and academic development.

---

*Special Note

I think it is very important to learn about the grieving child and also the effects of grief on a family. When you get a better understanding of this, you may be able to see how such an experience can affect the child's ability to learn at school. The grieving child is incredibly vulnerable to social and academic problems. It is important to remember that the grieving process does not have to be a process of dysfunction. Grief is a part of life. However, for children, such a loss is usually the first such traumatic experience. The more a child falls behind at school, the more difficult it is for them to catch up. These two factors alone are quite different than the adult experience of loss. Adults usually have more experience with loss, thus more coping skills. Adults also typically maintain a job or career as opposed to learning new material daily with subsequent testing.

A good team effort is necessary to assist these children in keeping their heads above water while their emotions drown and drain them. It is important to do everything possible so such a child is not retained as a result of conflicts/performance due to the loss. Retentions are difficult for many children to process, yet for these children it would typically be unnecessary and a constant reminder of the year of their loss. I believe connecting these two very difficult situations should be avoided at most costs. The school counselors and school nurse should play an active role in helping to monitor these children. Appetite and sleep problems are relatively common and could be addressed at school through arranged nap and healthy snack times. We can help them through tutoring and/or summer school as well. Human compassion should become the priority while the child regains their strength —strength needed for a journey through school years that require the cognitive, social, emotional energy necessary to both heal and attain overall school success.

More about grief and crisis is presented in Section III.

Your thoughts about step-parenting and schooling issues:

_____

_____

_____

_____

_____

_____

_____

_____

_____

_____

_____

_____

_____

YOUR THOUGHTS ON STEP-PARENTING: QUALITY OF RELATIONSHIP WITH EX-SPOUSE AND CHILDREN

The significant adults in the life of a child need to be part of the child's schooling when problems surface. When you entered into this adult relationship, were you aware of your spouse's children? Were they kept hidden from you throughout your courtship? Hopefully, you discussed parenting issues while you courted. You should not remove yourself from all parenting responsibility and the biological parent should also not attempt to thrust a primary parenting role upon you. There's a reasonable balance that must be communicated before you actually begin playing out this parenting teamwork. Don't forget, the other biological parent (under the better case scenarios) should continue to be a primary factor in this equation.

These issues create a challenging family make-up. I hope you discussed all these things prior to wedlock. If not, get started and consider seeking some professional support if you are not making any progress.

Next to consider are the interactions with the other biological parent. Do you demean that parent in front of the child? Do you demean them in ways you believe the child is unaware of? Do you believe the other parent does this to you? If this is not occurring on any level, pat yourselves and each other on the back. Unfortunately, in my experiences, non-occurrence of these negative behaviors is the exception. It usually takes quite an effort of patience and understanding by the step-parent and an emotionally mature spouse in order for a healthy relationship to occur between the step-parent and the child. If you, as a step-parent, engage in negative behavior by initiating it, by retaliating against the divorced parent, or by agreeing with a spouse's negative perspectives when in the presence of the child, your relationship with the child will be in much trouble.

The biological parent and the step-parent should have communicated about parenting issues prior to exposing the child or children to the relationship. If you did not discuss how you would team parent or had a weak, ambiguous parenting plan, it is crucial you both sit down immediately and begin this dialogue. You may have thought it will just work, but I have to tell you, it rarely, if ever, just works. It takes work.

_____

_____

_____

_____

_____

_____

Your thoughts on the numbers and/or variety of adults and children (other than intact family members) in a household as such factors relate to a child's schooling:

_____

_____

_____

_____

_____

_____

_____

_____

_____

_____

_____

_____

WHO RESIDES IN THE HOME

Who resides in the home? Other adults and children? The importance of the number and variety of household members is obvious. First, let us acknowledge the more adults in the home, the more likely adult and parenting egos will come into conflict, which in turn results in problems for the child/children. Such dynamics can create great instability and confusion in a child's life. Take a look at the relationships with these adults and your child. Are they close relatives, extended relatives, step-brothers, step sisters, friends, paramours? Do you have expectations of cooperative, supportive adult behaviors regarding modeling for your child? Are there expectations for teamwork with the child? Who takes the lead? When a conflict arises, who and how do the adults address it?

Why is this important in a discussion about children and school? This scenario lays the groundwork for how a child relates to adults who have authority roles yet are not the primary caregivers. Outside of the home, who are the people that have this role in the lives of most children? Teachers of course! Teachers can be the prime target of a child with anger and authority issues. This is not to say these issues cannot occur in an intact family without others in the home, but please understand the possibility for such problems greatly increase under the circumstances being discussed.

Did you address this before the household adult numbers expanded or a new adult entered the setting?

This is a very difficult issue for many parents living under such circumstances. You may reside with others or have others residing with you for a variety of reasons: financial challenges, housing problems, family issues, etc. No matter what the reason, you have to explore the necessity of such circumstances and you have to ask yourself if you considered the impact upon your child. If the impact is negative and these living conditions evolved due to poor decision-making, you must begin exploring appropriate, positive and healthy options. If you cannot see options, start by consulting with human services agencies to gain knowledge. It may take a few phone calls or trusting a friend to help.

Don't give up. Situations like these rarely resolve by themselves. If they do resolve *without any effort* or intervention by you, the *potential for it to occur again remains.* You must learn how to address and work through such a challenge to ensure it does not occur again.

It is very important that you understand bad things can happen when there are multiple adults and children living under one roof without role clarity and proper guidance and supervision. I'm not talking about a large family here, but rather situations where your children are surrounded by adult strangers or other children they may or may not know, whether they are relatives or not. Do these people have problems? What is the potential for positive vs. negative impact upon your child or children? Are these people positive influences? Are the adults good role models? What about other or older children? Are your children safe from abuses? There is no way such a situation will not impact upon a child's schooling in one way or another. Please do not be naïve enough to say everything is fine without processing the situation through listening and observing the environment you are now living in with your child. This kind of naiveté or denial takes courage to defeat; find it for your children. If you can answer these questions without any hesitation, one of three things may have happened:

1) You are fully aware and accountable for your child; 2) These issues are not important to you and you do not have the time or interest in this topic; or, 3) You are in significant denial.

I want to be direct, yet I also believe the latter two are now improbable since you have made a decision to read this material.

It is possible that a positive impact is occurring. If the reasons for this extended household were based upon the needs of your children they should appear happier, be working harder at school, having no school conflicts or reduced school conflicts, be mannerly with all adults (for the most part), and be sleeping and eating well. The positive signs are there to be seen, just as the negative signs are there if you choose to look. You will discover if these living arrangements are good or bad for your child through good observation and appropriate communication with the school. Don't blame the school for behaviors your child may be exhibiting if you have not addressed these issues.

_____

_____

_____

_____

_____

_____

_____

_____

_____

_____

_____

_____

_____

_____

_____

_____

Your thoughts regarding other caregivers such as extended relatives, foster care, residential staff and their roles in the schooling of children:

_____

_____

_____

_____

_____

_____

_____

_____

_____

_____

_____

_____

OTHER CAREGIVERS

If you are fully caring for a child and you are not one of the biological parents, the school needs documentation that legitimizes your role. This is presented through court documentation.

I believe the first thing you must acknowledge is that a child under these circumstances is going to have heightened emotional needs. There are always reasons these situations occur and they are rarely good from a child's perspective. You must ask yourself if you have fully recognized this. Even if the child's current life situation is good, there are feelings inside the child about his or her history and immediate family. The child's feelings on these matters should be monitored through healthy communication and observation.

Extended relatives, like grandparents who raise their children's children, appear to be presenting with increased frequency. Are you a foster care family? Are you a residential facility? Do you have temporary or permanent custody? Is there a possibility of parent-child reunification? It makes an incredible amount of uncommon sense to me that you understand the dynamics that challenge children in these situations.

Children in school are a reflection of the larger society and our larger society has significant issues that have altered over the years. Caregiver situations and arrangements have increased in variation. We have children in foster care that attend our schools and we have children who live in residential facilities who attend our schools. Residential and foster care settings are very much aware of the challenges children who reside with them face. Adults in these systems may also not understand how best to work with the school to address the child's overall needs. In order to help the child you must understand your role in the schooling process and you can learn this through good teamwork and communication with the school.

Wages within residential care settings are typically low and the job is incredibly difficult. Regardless, this should not be accepted as an excuse for poor work, but it often sets the groundwork for a high staff turnover rate, thus affecting consistency of relationships and consistency of school communication. Nonetheless, these people usually have a good understanding of the challenges they face with these children and also the challenges these children face for themselves. A primary issue, however, often goes unnoticed. Quite frequently the behaviors of these children can be so difficult and demanding that schooling issues become secondary. The reality is that these adults go into a survival-of-the-moment mode. This message is particularly relevant to staff in foster homes, residential treatment facilities and classrooms for children with emotional disturbances, to name a few.

I have recognized these children need to see a future that offers something better than their past. Schooling is about the future, while the draining survival mode only addresses present negative reactions to past bad experiences. It is easy to say we just want to make it through the day with certain children with severe behaviors or other problems. I implore you to recognize that the instillation of hope for a better future may be the most significant, meaningful, reinforcing real life tool you have just waiting to be used. Yes, you may need guidance with this strategy, so seek it. Seek it from your team, supervisor, therapist, or whatever way such feedback and knowledge may come, just seek it.

_____

_____

_____

_____

_____

_____

_____

_____

_____

_____

_____

_____

_____

_____

_____

_____

_____

_____

_____

_____

_____

_____

_____

_____

_____

_____

Your thoughts on bullying behaviors:

_____

_____

_____

_____

_____

_____

_____

_____

_____

_____

_____

_____

_____

_____

BULLYING BEHAVIORS

Please do not defend or deny bullying behaviors your child may be reported to exhibit. This issue is what actually prompted me to begin saying "our children". I want you to understand this is no longer just about you and your children. If your child has this problem, he or she is affecting other children and, therefore, their families as well. It is important to understand we all have a stake in the well-being of each other's children. And *it is our business,* because the behaviors of one child in a school can significantly affect the lives of the other children at school, for better or for worse. *It is all of our business.* If you have said in the past, "It's nobody else's business," I hope you will stop making such a statement.

Bad things again are going to happen unless you address the problem. Ultimately, someone *will* address the problem whether or not you choose to help with a solution. The outcomes are likely to be much more positive if you work with the school to help the child. By doing so, you will maintain control over the rearing of the child. If not, other systems may eventually take over and address the needs of your child. If this occurs, in retrospect, you will probably view the previous adults who did not mind their own business in a greatly different way. If you were to continue to be angry with them, then you are having much difficulty holding yourself accountable. It simply means it's just easier to keep focusing on something other than your own limitations. Take care of *your business* now so you can move forward with more confidence and peace. Children with bullying behaviors are worthy of just as much attention and help as those they bully; they're just easier to be angry at, even for adults.

_____

_____

_____

_____

_____

_____

_____

_____

_____

_____

_____

_____

_____

_____

Your thoughts on punishment:

_____

_____

_____

_____

_____

_____

_____

_____

_____

_____

_____

_____

_____

_____

PUNISHMENT CONCERNS

There seems a common inclination for many adults to rely on punishment to address behavior problems with children. This interests me because, again, uncommon sense must prevail. On a daily basis, parents and caregivers can confront and address numerous situations involving children and problems. You will burn yourself out if you consistently personalize. You may wonder why I say personalize. In my experiences, I have found punitive approaches are most often invoked because the adult addressing the situation feels the child has personally slighted them by misbehaving or by not producing a desired result. This is a greedy response. The problems are not always about the confronting adult, but punitive strategies usually are.

You may be doing something (within awareness or not) that promotes misbehavior, and as a parent, you must explore for this possibility. You must also know that misbehaviors are not always your fault. You may not always know what fosters anger or motivates your child to behave in certain ways. You can however, set limits with firmness and fairness while maintaining compassion for a child who obviously needs a different reaction other than angering another adult. For example, the child who appears to lie about everything, makes up stories, etc. Punitive strategies suggest you simply want these behaviors to cease. By taking that position you neglect or minimize the fact that the reasons for the behaviors are still a problem. Again, I'm not looking for deeper level clinical treatment here, but simple alternatives to punishment. Do children need to be held accountable for poor decisions? Certainly, but such decisions and the messages given along with them should be well-thought, connect to the behavior, and be followed through. It is the "following through" aspect of consequence enforcement in which caregivers usually falter. Be strong, seek assistance whenever possible, and have faith in yourself. When you sense yourself weakening think of the longer term results of enforcing, or not enforcing, limits with your children. This is not easy, though your parenting will become *easier* in time and a broader sense of success for your child's future will increase as well.

An alternative approach to punishment is one that considers the concept of logical consequences for all behaviors, be they pro-social or anti-social behaviors. I have observed children to react quite differently dependent on which term the adult uses or implies when attempting to discipline; "consequence" or "punishment". Children seem to associate a punishment more with something being given to them as opposed to something they deserved/earned. I did not say always because we know many children have said they deserved the punishment they received — at a later time and date of course.

However, when we are talking about a population of children who already have significant problems, something different occurs. Maybe it's because they have received so much attention for negative behaviors that they've conditioned themselves to believe punishment is something adults simply get a kick out of. There are also those children so hateful of themselves they appear to thrive on being punished because it reinforces their low self-esteem. This is a terrible circumstance to witness and, unfortunately, is not uncommon. We can say these are typical oppositional behaviors, denial, or whatever, but they do occur. I have found placing emphasis on the word "consequences" greatly diminishes resistance to personal accountability; maybe not immediately, but certainly over consistent use and time.

The earning of consequences for all behaviors is a far healthier concept to teach children than punishment. Consequences for one's actions teach internal control and internal control is a necessary foundation for personal responsibility and accountability. When we say to a child they have earned a consequence for a specific behavior, it is much different than saying I am punishing you for that behavior. This takes consistency and will-power on the adult's part because children who have been "punished" a lot struggle with the variation here. You have to keep saying, I'm not punishing you, *you earned* the consequence *for your* behavior/decision. This is a wonderful disciplinary tactic because its function is not merely one for future deterrence, as punishment seems to imply. It addresses the problem at hand while fostering or developing that internal sense of control we wish all humans to have, and it builds upon a respectful relationship. Remember, the discussion about fear-based classroom management and respect-based classroom management? A child's perception of punishment can promote an outcome similar to ongoing fear-based respondents — I will control my behavior only when I fear someone or only when I will be punished by someone.

We know that punishment can be fair and we know that punishment can be earned. However, with a portion of the children who are identified as having acting-out behavior problems in school, the way in which you approach discipline and the words you choose when disciplining matter.

I hope you recognize the concepts I mention are not loaded with clinical skills. I believe if a child's problems are to the point the school is concerned, parents or caregivers should consider external help. If school counseling is the only intervention occurring we run the risk of prompting the child to view the school as a treatment setting. The issues are then brought to the forefront of the child's psyche and he or she may lose the ability to focus on academic and social development while in school. There are times when this may be appropriate based on the individual needs of a child, but again such decisions should be weighed very carefully.

_____

_____

_____

_____

_____

_____

_____

_____

_____

_____

_____

_____

_____

_____

_____

_____

_____

_____

_____

_____

_____

_____

Your thoughts on the quiet/withdrawn child:

_____

_____

_____

_____

_____

_____

_____

_____

_____

_____

_____

_____

_____

THE QUIET/WITHDRAWN CHILD

This child is often a victim of their own behavior. It has been a challenge for me to foster the same level of concern for these children similar to the level of concern most feel for the acting out children. Uncommon sense tells us loud and clear that these children may also be experiencing problems. These children may be the recipients of bullying behaviors, may be suffering from some sort of abuse/ trauma, or they may be the children with attention deficit disorder, inattentive type, etc. Why then do we have a more difficult time and even resist accounting for them? Parents may misinterpret such behaviors as "shyness" or may not see what others report within the home setting. You must fight for objectivity when other people are suggesting you view your child's "shyness" as possibly something other than shyness.

There are children who are shy, but for our purposes we are looking at other possibilities. Different behavioral presentations occur because the structure of the family is different, relationships within the home are different and personality and parenting styles are different. Problems may evolve due to extremes of structure, relationships, parenting, or a variety of factors. There are almost always very clear reasons why children behave differently in general and different in specific situations. When such a presentation does not seem to have a practical reason or is presenting problems for your child in some aspect of their life it is time for professional assistance. They may appear well-mannered (because they are not creating any conflict). Their low grades may be explained and defended by lower ability level since they are never causing a problem; they always appear to be listening or focused. We know such problems exist and we must be on the look-out for it. These children may be more vulnerable to very bad things than children who act out.

Internalizing pain and anger does terrible things to our bodies, minds and hearts and it goes on in our world and homes everyday. We don't like it when a child acts out and we certainly don't want to see anyone hurt. How different are these children that are everyday beating themselves from within? We can typically hear and see the acting out child serving notice that they need help. The child who internalizes does not call out for help in the same way, but the call is still being made, but in a different manner.

_____

_____

_____

_____

_____

_____

_____

Your thoughts on the issue of racism (you may ponder other "isms" as well):

_____

_____

_____

_____

_____

_____

_____

_____

_____

_____

_____

_____

_____

RACISM CONCERNS

We should know that exposure is key for humans to understand and accept each other's differences. This is not just about races and color. We are so weird. A price is paid when such lessons go unlearned and these lessons go unlearned everyday. We appear for maybe some anthropologically defined reasons to resist and sometimes even despise difference and change. We have not recognized that this has little to do with color and race, and more to do with anything different/unfamiliar. Unfortunately, color is so visible and we've caused so much damage in the name of skin color for so long, it is taking a long time to let it go, heal and move forward as humans together.

A school would be remiss to believe that they have no issues of racism to be concerned with. Unfortunately, as long as there are any children of minority status in the school, there will likely be some form of racism. This does not mean outward nastiness occurs all the time. A strange phenomenon occurs when there are only a few minority children in a school and they happen to be well-liked. These minority children become the exception to the rule. People can afford to say these are "good ones" because they are not yet perceived as threatening their way of life. Watch what happens to the same community when the number of minority persons increase. Fear begins to set in and often without reason or provocation.

There are times when fear is appropriate, but we have to be clear of its origin. For example, let's say there is a 100% African American community and a Caucasian family moves in with drug dealing motives. The easy way out for a racist attitude would be to focus on the color. The color isn't going to jump off their face and hurt you, but their drugs, violence and weaponry that can come with it may.

For a school or school district that has not been exposed to a larger segment of a minority population, the probability for racist attitudes appears to significantly increase. The effects of non-exposure have created the illusion that the born and raised residents are the better humans and they can only be damaged should a minority population enter their utopia. But you know what? It has not been utopia. There have likely been prior feuds or problems in this town due to some people thinking and doing things differently. All things being equal, color included, we will find things different in each other. Some people will feel they are fortunate to be able to tag that "different" label on a group of people in order to gain some sort of power or status in the community. Read the Dr. Seusse story about the Star Belly Sneetches for a childhood lesson on this matter.

It's not about color; we've made it about color. Terrible decisions about color have been made for a very long time simply because it's an obvious difference. Understanding and accepting difference is a normal part of a healthy life. If you are not grasping this, simply observe children in groups. Watch how they pick, choose, and base decisions upon friendships, especially around the age of nine through sixteen or so. Developing children have developing egos and many, at times, will see differences as negative in other children in order to massage and develop their own egos. Most are not doing this because they are inherently cruel; they are simply trying to find their place. They are learning about relationships; differences, patience, compassion, and conflict resolution and adults are their models. If there are no adults muddying the waters with hurtful attitudes about our brothers and sisters of difference (this goes well beyond color), children will come through this without issues of racism or other "isms".

I frequently ask adults to explore their feelings about other races. What I often find are people either willing to alter their beliefs, people in denial (who have been noted to present comments/behaviors indicative of racism) or people simply refusing to change beliefs. I challenge you to ask yourself where you stand. My response to people who have these feelings in their hearts is this: I believe one loses their self-given right to condemn another human if they have in any way added to the problem he or she is condemning. So, if you live with these hurtful beliefs and you impart your beliefs to children, you should lose the right to complain or judge any other human being's behavior. I know an enforcement issue presents here, but if people consistently bring this viewpoint to the violator's attention maybe he or she will eventually "get it". Silence can bring good things, but in this situation it brings the perception of approval.

Sadly, it appears quite difficult for people who exhibit these behaviors to understand this life lesson, yet some do. I realize we cannot "make" people stop, but the more people not accepting of these behaviors, the more likely the change. Please know if you don't say anything when you hear such comments, you are tacitly approving. Hearts and minds are affected by non-acceptance in larger numbers. This does not mean to fight with people, just disagree with their comments. If they want to have a rational dialogue wonderful, if not, just move on. It's because of this behavior that this terrible issue is hanging around! It's kind of like non-voters. Don't complain about our political leaders if you did not take part in the decision-making process. You should lose that right by not using your right.

Some people appear to celebrate differences and not always with a joyous heart. We continue to acknowledge little of our similarities, of which there are far more, while our commonalities have the potential to take us to better places if we could see more of ourselves in each other. Most of us seem to give *a difference* the same power as one negative comment in a day of a thousand positives.

_____

_____

_____

_____

_____

_____

_____

_____

_____

_____

_____

_____

_____

_____

_____

Special Note:

The previous four areas discussed (bullying, withdrawn behaviors, punishment and racism/isms) really challenge your ability to self-assess. You have to consider reviewing your parenting to see if you are in fact contributing to a child's challenges in these areas. If you became defensive during this section you have something you may choose to address for the betterment of you and most importantly your child's life. He or she is worth your honest assessment and if need be, your commitment to change. Remember, I don't want you beating yourself up about these issues, nor do I wish you to invalidate all the good parenting things you have done. You are human and since being so, you are vulnerable to all the anger, mixed messages, and media portrayals handed down or bestowed upon you by your history in this world. You have the opportunity to change. You've always had the opportunity to change. Hopefully, your child's future will be the motivational force behind such change. If this occurs, please thank him or her at some point.

Your thoughts on the parenting role of a child receiving
or being considered for special education services:

_____

_____

_____

_____

_____

_____

_____

_____

_____

_____

_____

_____

_____

SPECIAL EDUCATION CONCERNS

All that has been said to this point is now magnified ten fold for teachers, caregivers and your child. Your role significantly increases when the problem either warrants a child's consideration of special education services or has qualified and is receiving them. This child may be exhibiting high needs in one or many areas. They may have a learning disability, a low level of cognitive ability, an emotional disturbance, a brain injury, speech and language deficits, or have one or more of a variety of clinical disorders (e.g. autism, attention deficit disorder) that prompt consideration and possible need for special education services. There are no rules about the mixture of these issues. Just as a child can have a learning disability and an attention deficit disorder, he or she can also be classified as functioning in the mental retardation range and also have an attention deficit disorder.

There is an infinite range of complex interactions that affect the basic functioning and development of humans. Weeding out such issues is no easy task and sometimes may not be fully possible due to communication problems the child may have. Nonetheless, the challenge of appropriate diagnostic information demands a higher level of investment from both the home and school district. The labels mentioned should only come after the best teamwork possible has not been able to meet the child's specific behavioral and/or academic needs, and the label has diagnostic credibility that will provide direction for intervention.

Unfortunately, this population of children seems to be most vulnerable to the "blame game". Who is responsible for what? It really is a simple answer—we all are. The challenge becomes the specificity of, and accountability for, what each member of the team is expected to do. By simply being placed within special education should not be readily perceived as better, or as the best alternative. Without good rationale and teamwork, this placement can be a disaster. We now have a child who will be challenged by the label in which they qualified for such services. Though some would like to minimize this "labeling" issue, I cannot. It is not just how the child perceives the label, but how adults perceive labels as well. The key word here is "expectations". We lose control over the inherent beliefs the adults in the child's life now, or in the future, have regarding labels and expectations. Everyone on the team should be very clear on the expectations of the child. They have to be realistic, yet challenging to the child. The expectations cannot be decreased out of lack of faith and hope for significant success; and again, define success. With exceptional teamwork the child will quite often exceed expectations. I often tell parents and teachers there is no way to measure the child's heart. There is no way to initially guarantee what will motivate the child to move beyond adult-placed expectations. This is a beautiful process when it unfolds because it affirms the power of teamwork and the inner spirit of those involved, in particular, the child.

I would also like to make a comment about "Gifted Programming". I always want parents and teachers to understand the result of any label no matter how the label is perceived. I talk to parents about the *possible* repercussions of a "Gifted" label. How the child internalizes the label, how peers perceive the label and what adults do with the label. You can rest assured that perceptions will change from pre to post labeling. I encourage parents and teachers to observe for balance of social and academic achievement. I advocate all to recognize a child's need to experience fun, laughter and silliness. I try to help parents and teachers learn how to communicate a healthy balance to such a child. This child may need instructional enrichments to have academic challenges, yet social needs cannot go unmet and such needs are sometimes even "punished". For example, when reprimands and expressions of disappointment are placed upon the child for socializing prior to an exam and *only* a score of 90 percent is earned. These challenges may come from many directions for this child and possibly even be self-induced. This child will likely need coping skill assistance when, and if, a peer says, "You think you're better than me, don't you?" or, "You're weird!" These comments can hurt just as much as the comments put out there to children with learning problems.

Don't kid yourself, labels are a big issue and we must be ready to help the child through such challenges. The self-esteem of a child is at great risk. Though it may have been low prior to identification, it can get lower. Please do not misunderstand me; I believe when a label is truly warranted and the team considers all angles, communicates well and attends to the child's spirit, good things happen. Appropriate planning can raise the esteem of a child if true placement is necessary. Educating them about their disability is crucial to help them re-establish a learning foundation. They can become stronger and the issue of negative peer and even adult perception is greatly minimized. Remember, the goal continues to be to educate the child to his or her fullest potential. In order to do so, the building blocks for self-confidence and esteem must be an integral part of this child's educational programming.

A special challenge arises when a child tested for the aforementioned services does not qualify to receive them. What happens then? The problems were significant enough to proceed with the evaluation process so they should be addressed regardless of qualification outcome. I believe a child should never be tested to simply answer the "Qualify or Not" question. I believe a child should be evaluated to determine how best to meet his or her needs regardless of the "Qualification" status. A good evaluation will almost always uncover causal rationales for the child's lack of progress regardless of qualification status. The child's emotional, social, or academic needs must be met whether in a special education classroom or regular education classroom. Much progress can be made in regular educational settings that develop good teamwork habits and that also promote good evaluations to guide them in their efforts.

The challenge is now to get the team (child included when appropriate) on the same page in order to address the problems from a different viewpoint. Simply by being tested, every child will not qualify for specialized instruction, yet the child should believe that something is going to change for the better. Qualification standards and evaluation procedures are often misunderstood or questioned, but it is what schools currently practice through state and federal guidelines. But, if qualification status is not your primary concern and helping the child regardless of the "qualify or not" outcome, then the outcome status loses its formerly attributed power.

Another important factor to acknowledge regards private evaluations. Private evaluations can be quite different from those conducted by the school district. A private evaluation may make a diagnosis of a learning problem and recommend special education services, yet the school's evaluation may disagree. Private evaluators are usually not privy to, or possibly not concerned with, state guidelines for special education identification criteria. For example, a child may have a learning disability on paper, yet his or her academic history suggests he or she has learned how to compensate for it. Learning may still challenge the child, yet specialized services are not deemed necessary.

There sometimes appears a belief that the school district is out to avoid special education placements based on a private practitioner's evaluation. This may be fueled by frustrated, angry parents or inappropriate advocacy, especially if the school does not believe such a placement is warranted and the family does. On the other hand, a school's perception may be that the private practitioner is being rewarded quite well financially for their evaluation and they will continue testing until a problem is observed. The private practitioner or advocate may also not be aware of caregiver issues that have hampered the child's academic, social and emotional development. The school district may also say a learning problem of some sort may be found in most people with continued extensive testing, even "A" and "B" grade performers. These children, however, have learned how to compensate for it. Children who are affected by significant learning disabilities for whatever reason have not been able to compensate for their deficit areas. Without good communication between the school and the private evaluator the private evaluation may not have considered the child's academic history, teacher feedback, or the state guidelines that warrant such a placement. A good private evaluation will include relevant school and family information.

This issue also has the potential to set up adversarial relationships between the home and school and again, it is often the result of poor communication. Ultimately, what may happen is the child being placed inappropriately in special education for factors that may have been addressed through regular education with "reasonable accommodations". With the child as the primary benefactor, the team should always specify and mandate such accommodations. Good communication between private and school evaluators will address the criteria for placement. The fact is both reports may provide excellent information. A team determined to help the child without *professional ego interruptus* will do just that—help the child.

Perhaps placement guidelines do need thoughtful reconsideration, but this will probably not occur if the diagnostic team (regular education personnel being teachers, principals and vice-principals; special education personnel being teachers, directors, supervisors; school psychologists and other professional evaluators; guidance counselors, school social workers, school nurses and parents) does not work together to reach a common good—a good based upon the needs of children. Together, school boards, professional associations and politicians can be educated about the practical needs of all students. Apart, we simply invite these people to become part of the "blame game" and this appears attractive to some because it redirects responsibility and accountability. Fighting the "good fight" takes courage and a willingness to take a hit. We will not always choose the best methods to help the child and the child will not always make acceptable progress. I'd rather take a hit with a great team as this assures the fight to continue, while the blamers argue/fight with whomever. A great team will reassess and begin moving forward with the child's best interests in mind again. Historically, all great teams have had this characteristic and they most likely became great because of it.

Special Note

The issue of behavioral accountability for children with Individual Education Plans (IEPs) has reached many a conference table. I implore people to recognize all children must be accountable for their actions. In these cases, the team has to assure it had done everything stated in the IEP to help the child. If there were behavioral issues building, but not addressed in the IEP that could be a problem. If academic interventions in the IEP were not implemented appropriately that could be a problem. Regardless, an acting-out behavior of a child still must be addressed. For example, a child pushes a desk over because the teacher pushed the child with a reading disability to read in front of the class. The teacher not only needs to make amends appropriately, but the child should be required to pick the desk back up and apologize to the class for the disruption. The team may consider helping the child explain his/her frustrations to the class and the teacher may need help in explaining his/her role in this incident. These are sensitive areas and definitely require team involvement and decision-making.

In the event that a child hurts another child or adult, I almost always want the school and parent to consider suspension (in-school or out-of-school) and possible expulsion. The last thing the school, parents or caregivers should want to do is present the appearance that such behavior is tolerated because of the child's disability. Now, there are obvious needs here to be case-specific. Nonetheless, I believe the rules have been greatly manipulated through poor advocacy, lawyers not looking out for the best interests of children, parents not able to recognize the potential damage from lack of accountability, and schools not appropriately addressing the behavioral, social and emotional needs of children who have low-frustration tolerance.

An example that comes to mind is the child that has learned or perceives the school or teacher cannot discipline him/her. After an inappropriate behavior gets him sent to the office he is immediately sent back to the class. He boldly walks in and sarcastically smirks at the teacher, thus with all the nonverbal (sometimes verbal) power possible identifies himself as "untouchable and unaccountable". Ladies and gentlemen, I want all to know when the situation evolves to this degree the future of this child is at great risk. This is not a time to banter about what the school cannot do or how angry the parents are with the school or teacher. Do what is right and in the best interests of the child and clean up any other garbage afterwards.

When did it become inappropriate for an adult to apologize to a child openly (in front of a class)? When did it become inappropriate to hold all children accountable for their actions? When did it become inappropriate for a child to apologize to his/her classmates for inappropriate behaviors? Yes, we sometimes have to hold some children accountable in different ways, yet somehow the consequence must match the behavior. School Districts with skillful understanding of these issues, excellent communication with teachers and parents of all children, and exceptional Parent-Teacher Associations will address these concerns with integrity.

_____

_____

_____

_____

_____

_____

_____

_____

_____

_____

_____

_____

_____

_____

_____

_____

_____

_____

*Special Note

Children having problems need to see hope in the eyes of the adults that surround them. Children are incredibly perceptive to truth and hope. Be careful not to patronize them and caution yourself to insincere compliments. Only say things you truly feel and be careful not to say it too frequently; it may lose its intended power.

Do not be surprised if your child does not initially respond favorably to positive messages. The child may actually continue to pursue a conflict despite the positive energy. I have found several probable reasons for these reactions and they are not uncommon. First, he or she may simply believe it's a forced strategy to "get them to do better". Second, they may test the adults to see if they are sincere with their commitment to this new process. Or third, they may experience an increase in pressure toward academic, social, or behavioral expectations, which may in turn increase the child's anxiety level. You just have to continue. Be supportive, yet develop and/or maintain limits. Try not to overreact to pessimistic comments from the child; at this stage they may truly believe they are not capable of positive change. Let them see your hope and renewed commitment to them. When the child perceives the positive energy as stronger than his/her negative energy good things are more apt to happen.

_____

_____

_____

_____

_____

_____

_____

_____

_____

_____

_____

_____

_____

_____

*Special Note

Parents and Caregivers, when your child has a clinical diagnosis to which medication management has been a typical treatment approach, I would like you to understand the following. The teacher, counselor, school psychologist, principal or district personnel cannot coerce you to use such an approach. Certainly everyone has opinions, but this decision is yours to make. However, I do want you to consider this - many clinical disorders appear to require the combination of medication management and talk therapy in order to meet with success. The challenge comes, however, when a decision to not use medication management is made and no other treatment is implemented. Clinical disorders require treatment. If you choose not to use medication management for your child's depression, anxiety, or attention deficit you must choose another treatment with your doctor. Should you simply tell the school, "We will not put our child on meds" the school has the right to ask "So how have you decided to treat him or her?" Good school personnel cannot sit idly by while a child's clinical disorder goes untreated—this is not just about medication. Not having a treatment alternative may create problems for you with social services and it will definitely create more problems for your child. Please have a plan developed to treat your child's disorder appropriately. Your child's doctor should be able to provide you with alternative treatments. If not, the school counselor, nurse or school psychologist may be able to provide some other resources for you.

In summary, the severity of specific disorders often receives the most benefit from medication. The research and many professionals may tell you this, yet your belief system will not allow it. I encourage you to consider the possible outcomes without appropriate intervention. If the child is not "getting better" and he or she is not experiencing success at school or probably elsewhere, will you be frustrated and possibly *even angry at the school? Schools are run by people and they can only do so much. Severe clinical disorders frequently offer more challenges than most school personnel are trained for and/or are able to deal with successfully. Under these circumstances you must also be consulting with professionals outside of the school setting.*

_____

_____

_____

_____

_____

_____

_____

_____

_____

_____

_____

_____

_____

_____

_____

_____

_____

_____

_____

_____

_____

_____

_____

_____

_____

Your thoughts about parental/caregiver responsibility for contact between home and school:

RESPONSIBILITY FOR HOME-SCHOOL CONTACT

The trap that appears to occur when a child is having difficulty at school (especially when acting out behaviors are involved) is one of negative reinforcement. The calls may come frequently from either direction and they can rapidly spiral out of control and simply turn into defensive battles. If it has gotten to this point I would be quite confident in saying the teamwork has since broken down. Common sense tells us communication is necessary, yet uncommon sense tells us it must remain goal oriented and positive, despite the level of frustration being experienced by you and the teacher/s. I think you may have recognized the belief that if you maintain an open and positive relationship with your child's teacher good things usually happen for the child.

I believe a positive scenario is rarely possible without a foundation built on solid communication. If the child has exhibited signs of school difficulties over the years, you should have been, or must now consider, mending fences and developing such a foundation. The fact the relationship may have deteriorated may not be your fault, however, partial responsibility is yours if it has remained negative. There is a mutual responsibility to communicate appropriately to help a child struggling at school. You, and certainly not your child, can afford to have communication ties severed with the school or school district.

You are also encouraged to explore a relationship with your child's guidance counselor. A good guidance counselor is a gold mine for any school or child. Most are overwhelmed with paperwork demands and wear many different hats. I believe they will make time for you and go that famous extra mile if you are committed to your child's educational experience. If your child has the potential for interaction with the vice principal, I also suggest you explore that relationship. Again, if you exhibit a commitment to your child's educational experience, this person will likely respond in favor. Be patient with these school personnel as they typically deal with many challenges with many children on a daily basis. Your efforts to become a team player will be noted, and then you will have to sustain that effort. This is how mutual respect is developed on such teams. Behaviors will almost always prove stronger than words.

If you have ceased communicating with the school you must understand a seldom used tool to mandate your involvement. A review of child abuse law will lead you to a list of varying kinds of child abuse. One of the types of abuse listed may be "educational neglect" in some states or possibly "neglect" in general in most states. Again, this is seldom acknowledged or pursued, but I do advocate for it under extreme circumstances. How might it get to this point? It could be frustration, it could be a perceived sense of negative judgment from school personnel, or it could actually be a belief that any child's issue in the school is the school's problem. Some parents appear to believe their involvement with *their* child's education is optional and some do not present this philosophy with malicious intent. Pressured involvement doesn't always make for appropriate involvement, but it does present an opportunity to repair an embattled history or to develop a new relationship between home and school because at least you are now all at the same table.

I've had very positive meetings addressing such issues with parents. Some sincerely believed the school was supposed to take care of all problems while the child was under their care. If a child is having significant problems such involvement is not optional. All of these issues are workable and changeable. Something has to give; to continue on a course of separateness will most likely guarantee failure for the child across a spectrum of domains and academics is just one. I do not believe you would allow this to occur because of your decision to gain knowledge. You may get so frustrated, tired, or angry that the severing of ties with the school may seem an appealing option. Think it through—it would only seem appealing because you're angry, you're tired and you're frustrated. What would not be acknowledged are your child's needs. There may be times when it would be appropriate to step away for a little while in order to regain some positive energy. If this is the case, share it with someone you communicate with at the school. If you have a reputation that prompts the school to question your sincerity then again you must challenge yourself to a truthful self-assessment. The energy spent to develop good relationships and teamwork with your child's school and teacher is well worth it and your efforts will be noted.

It is not typically a good idea, or appropriate, to fully depend on a child (age irrelevant) to relay adult messages, either by word or backpack. Decisions to do this must involve a team dialogue that accounts for all the specific variables related to the issue in question.

_____

_____

_____

_____

_____

_____

_____

_____

_____

_____

_____

_____

_____

_____

_____

_____

Your thoughts regarding teamwork and commitment:

_____

_____

_____

_____

_____

_____

_____

_____

_____

_____

_____

_____

_____

TEAMWORK AND COMMITMENT

There is no substitute. There is little alternative. I guess it's possible to go without these factors in other areas of life, but certainly not when working with children having problems. I'll simplify it further and say not with children, period. Again, some parents, teachers, caregivers may believe they can "go it alone" or tell others to mind their own business when it comes to addressing a child's problems from a team perspective. The problems of one child have an impact upon other children who are connected in some way. A child will either bring friendship, joy, trust, compassion to those connected, or they will bring hostility, sadness, worry, fear, and mistrust. One way or another each child has an impact upon others. This is most important in the school setting because the classroom system functions on the team concept. Just as one child can energize a class by his or her wit, humor, pro-social skills, so can the child impact the class with disruption and fear.

I have recognized the need for these children to see a future that offers something better than their past. Schooling is about the future, while the draining survival mode only addresses present negative reactions to past bad experiences. It is easy to say we just want to make it through the day with certain children having significant problems. I implore you to recognize that the instillation of hope for a better future may be the most significant, meaningful, reinforcing, clinical, everyday-life-tool you have just waiting to be used. Yes, you may need guidance with this strategy, so seek it. Seek it from your team, supervisor, counselor, school nurse or whoever. Keep searching for whatever way such feedback and knowledge may come — just seek it.

I believe educating a higher need child is a great challenge which does not come easy; it's not supposed to. Good parents and teachers will always challenge themselves and they will appropriately challenge the child. The broader assessment of a teacher and a school's character may be best measured by the level of success children with difficult challenges experience. For parents, it may be in your willingness to make difficult decisions and support the team's effort to help your child.

Special Note:

Caregivers, homework time is a critical element to helping the identified child be successful academically. It is frequently a primary focal point that is totally under your control; home investment in this area is key. Problems in this area will inevitably sabotage the school's commitment to the child. School personnel can assist with developing a homework plan, yet the caregivers are ultimately the one's to carry it out. You must be certain and confident with your role and you must be clear about the teacher's expectations. If not, ask questions. You may not understand all the academic tasks the child needs to do, yet you can set up the most optimal environment with fair and firm expectations. Success in this area has a high probability of transferring to behavior, social and emotional success also. Again, these issues are rarely mutually exclusive.

Your thoughts on Home-Schooling Children:

_____

_____

_____

_____

_____

_____

_____

_____

_____

_____

_____

_____

_____

_____

THE ISSUE OF HOME-SCHOOLING CHILDREN

This is a hot topic these days. Parents certainly have this right, but I believe parents should view this as more of a privilege. I want all parents who are home-schooling their children, or are considering it, to ask themselves the following questions:

Do I have the skills to educate/teach my child?

Are my concerns for public education and/or schooling outside of my home founded?

Am I separating my history and/or my issues from the current life and schooling experiences of my child?

Have I shared my concerns with the home school district?

I have met wonderful parents who made this choice and their children are happy, learning and socially adept with peers and adults. When done with the utmost care about academic and social balance it can work. However, I have also seen children hurt by home-schooling for ill-thought reasons; i.e., parent issues. Minimal teaching skill level and no attention to academic and social balance have been observed in such situations. It is because of these cases that I truly believe this option should have better oversight. This may not be a popular view with parents, but my opinions are not based upon maintaining good graces with everyone, but on looking out for the needs of our children. I believe most parents will be able to assess and consider my concerns.

Ultimately, our public and private schools must truly listen to your concerns and address issues that are prompting families to consider and engage in this option.

———————————————————————————————

———————————————————————————————

———————————————————————————————

———————————————————————————————

———————————————————————————————

———————————————————————————————

———————————————————————————————

———————————————————————————————

———————————————————————————————

———————————————————————————————

———————————————————————————————

_____

_____

_____

_____

_____

_____

_____

_____

_____

_____

_____

_____

_____

_____

_____

_____

Your thoughts on renewing your commitment to be the best parent or caregiver for your child:

_____

_____

_____

_____

_____

_____

_____

_____

_____

_____

_____

_____

_____

BEGINNING OR RENEWING YOUR COMMITMENT

It would be beneficial for you to write down one to three issues you wish to address concerning your child's current schooling challenges and be specific. Next, write down the first steps you want to take in each area to begin the process. Then, identify your team members and make an appointment to discuss teamwork and role responsibilities. You may need support and guidance as you make your first attempt. If you have a good relationship with a relevant professional at the school, you may want to consider having this person assist in the development and process of the meeting. If not, you may take a risk and trust whomever the school refers for assistance in scheduling such a meeting. And finally, mentally prepare to resist the urge to give up, especially when setbacks occur. Remember, your child's problems have most likely been around for a while and they're going to take a while to change for the better. One possible timeline to assess for progress is report card periods. Increases in grades, pro-social skills/behaviors and attendance are usually well tracked on elementary school report cards. For middle and high school age children, the social and behavioral issues may have to be assessed through other means.

1) Issue:

Step I:

2) Issue:

Step I:

3) Issue:

Step I:

A Few Summary Points

Again, this material is not intended to include all possible problems you may encounter in your teaching of children. Your passion to teach/parent will afford you new information and the opportunity to explore and experiment with new strategies everyday.

It is also time to recognize that children's needs, regardless of severity, should no longer be viewed as automatically moving toward the path of special education. The "Response to Intervention" model (also known as the Problem Solving Model) is designed to assist children with significant learning challenges in regular education through teamwork across professional disciplines within the school setting. This model can merge special and regular education the way it may prove most useful and successful for children. Should this movement take hold across our public school systems, the percentage of children receiving special education labels and services should significantly decrease. Special education labels would no longer be required to assist children with intensive needs. Short-term intensive services may be implemented and last through a school year. Such an intervention could be provided with teamwork from **all** teachers and other service providers. This model has the potential to truly protect children from unnecessary and/or inappropriate placements. The primary goal of such a system is to help children bring their academic (reading most frequently) levels up to, or near, their same grade level peers. This would be an intensive intervention well spent if the child's academic struggles are resolved and they can move forward with more typical academic instruction and pace.

In the case where significant progress is not indicated, the validity and appropriateness of special education services may be determined to be in the best interests of the child. It will be wise for you to begin educating yourself about these systems, though not new in concept, they are gaining ground across the nation.

_____

_____

_____

_____

_____

_____

_____

All that being said,

WELCOME

TO

THE

GOOD FIGHT!

Section III

SCHOOLS, CRISES, AND LESSONS GAINED FROM 9/11

School crisis and the post 9/11 schooling world

The beginning of the 2001-2002 school year began with a tragedy that will likely be recognized as altering the course of world history. This subject has since evolved into extreme matters of partisan politics, religious conflicts, immigration issues and belief systems. The battle of good versus evil has come home in a manner never before experienced in the United States of America. I think we can agree this has had a significant impact within the public school system. At the time there was little clarity as to how we were to discuss the topics of terrorism, political partisanship, and religious expression.

So there we were. All these topics coming up in school everyday and I don't believe many, if any, school systems had adopted well-thought policies as to how best confront these issues. Teachers were being presented with these issues in their classes and school support staffs were being challenged to address problems associated with children's fears. If we are honest with ourselves and each other, I don't believe we have yet truly processed how we, as a nation, must communicate with children about these very difficult issues.

During that school year I was employed by a school district in northeastern Pennsylvania. This school district had been challenged by a significant amount of loss prior to and during the 2001-2002 school year. We had a young child die of rapid onset leukemia, a father killed in a tragic lightning accident with many children and friends in witness and we lost children through terrible vehicle accidents. It was all we could do to support our grieving families, friends of the deceased and school personnel. And through it all, from 9/11/01 and forward, these losses were coinciding with a rapidly changing and scary world. Many of our parents, children and teachers were asking for help and many who were not, probably should have been. They either did not recognize how these losses and 9/11 were taking a toll on them or they were resistant to admit any needs.

In February of 2002, I wrote much of what I will speak of in this section and had it approved by the director of special education and superintendent. Per the support of the special education director I had also done a couple of PTA presentations to discuss these issues.

The following information is what I have to offer should you strive toward a more guided/informed effort when dealing with such tragedies in local and world events.

We seem to have lost a common identity. Despite what many think, I do believe in this country even with so much ethnic diversity we can still have commonality as citizens of the United States of America. I believe good citizenship has to have a very clear sense of commonality that unites us. I think this premise is inherent in the word citizenship—to be a part of something and to be accountable to ourselves and each other.

I think it is incredibly important for our children to feel safe and have their anxiety levels within normal ranges in order to learn. They need to be well rested and emotionally stable in order to reach their maximum learning potential when they enter our schools. And we cannot forget about being supportive to parents. Parents must know how we are dealing with these issues and they must know what the school expects of them in order for their children to learn. We must also take care of our teachers and all school personnel, while our school leaders must take care of each other.

First of all, I believe you must acknowledge your own feelings about our nation's challenges. Children have an uncanny ability to see through insincere words/acts, and are quite adept at hearing what is not being said. Honesty in communication is important. What complicates this, however, is being honest about fears and concerns, while also instilling security and hope. When we recognize the complexity of this task then we must understand that we must speak to children at their age and maturity levels. All of this is difficult and there is not "one way". I do not expect all school personnel and parents to be therapists, yet there are simple ways to communicate with children about these issues that can promote unity, thus enhance the peace and strength we want to project onto **our** children. We can do this, but to have the most positive and powerful impact we must do this together. If you falter you have to know how to re-energize. And you will likely falter at some point simply by virtue of being human.

Crisis support teams are sometimes ill-defined and not fully understood by all school district personnel or parents.

A good crisis support team is aware of the need to separate clinical issues from normal life challenges within the school setting. When our children experience crisis in the school setting or the crisis makes its way into the school setting, the team's main task is to re-establish a sense of normalcy and routine as quickly and appropriately as possible. This team understands the longer normalcy and routine are disrupted the more difficult it becomes to reestablish. The process of having children sent to the guidance office has typically been well thought out. In that setting we can assist many children experiencing crisis for their first time. This also gives the team the opportunity to observe students for their coping skill levels and to help determine who is at risk for varying conflicts. For most children, compassionate messages from adults and being with some of their friends to process initial shock is most helpful. This process is not therapy. This is counseling and support.

There is a huge difference between counseling and therapy. The latter is quite clinical in nature and usually involves in-depth longer-term treatment. When clinical needs do evolve, the appropriate school personnel will assess the individual's needs and develop a plan with the intent the family will pursue external assistance. Grieving children and children dealing with such fears as terrorism do not always necessitate therapy. This is a very important concept to understand. Most people can move through such issues with good support systems and some supplemental counseling/guidance. This kind of counseling involves discussing normal feelings associated with such events and practical ways to deal with them. Therapy becomes a possibility or necessity when someone does not exhibit healthy coping skills. Or, some folks have other significant issues going on in their life which interferes with their ability to deal appropriately with or heal from traumatic events.

It is very important that all children who seek support receive it, even if you believe a child is not experiencing any distress, yet is simply going with the flow or taking advantage of the situation to get out of class. When a person seeks attention and utilizes a situation in this way it may indicate a problem the support team should be aware of. This issue reminds me of a conflict during my clinical training as a graduate student. I was treating a young lady who reported experiencing multiple personalities and had, in fact, been previously diagnosed with the disorder. My program included nine doctoral students. Three believed in the disorder and the other five did not. I believed there was clinical value to whatever your argument. Regardless of clinician opinion, the fact a person was telling you they were experiencing multiple personalities is a problem in itself, even if "acting". The point —— we often learn a lot about people whether their pain presents as sincere or theatrical, and sometimes those who present with theatrics need significant clinical attention too. Those who seek to take advantage of such a situation for some kind of personal gain, i.e., time out of class, are making one heck of a statement about their own conscience. These individuals may also need a level of clinical attention for such behaviors.

When stressed or fearful, people can become vulnerable to behave more differently than usual. Some people may become more irritable, some more withdrawn, and some may simply state all is great. We may be better served through awareness of how stress and/or fear affect us and how this may then impact upon those around us. This may also help us be more understanding of others around us when difficult times arise. This does not mean to tolerate abusive behavior, yet it does mean to consider the person may not be behaving in a way to specifically conflict with you.

During crisis, you should consider ways for people to have personal space when frustrated and then follow through by talking about the situation/behavior with them afterwards. This concept is important in all relationships; husband-wife, teacher-student, employee-employer, etc. Please acknowledge the following. When addressing the needs of **our** children it becomes even more important to maintain consistency of fair behavioral expectations with fair and logical limits and consequences. This consistency, despite what a child states verbally, provides stability which is greatly needed during times of crisis. This is not the time to "let things slide". In fact, if this occurs on any significant level the inconsistency will destabilize and present more problems for all involved. The results of whatever path is chosen have long since played out in families, relationships, classrooms and schools for either healthy or unhealthy outcomes. Yes, children may become angry, but when you are fair and include them in a dialogue about behavioral expectations, limits and consequences, they'll likely get over it. If they don't, then it is highly probable there are deeper issues manifesting.

The challenge with terrorism and its effect upon us is how much power we attribute to it or how much power we allow it to take from us. How we cope with this depends in large upon one's previously developed coping skills. I would like you to consider that as adults we typically have experienced more traumatic events simply by virtue of time (usually). Such experiences have afforded us the opportunity to develop our coping skills. Therefore, the older one is the more likely he/she is better able to cope with crisis (not necessarily, but more probable). We become so important because **our** children are not automatically equipped to deal effectively with traumatic events so they will look to us. They will watch how we cope with the loss of **our** children, they will watch us to see how we cope with terrorism threats, and they will study us not just for a short period of time, but for the long haul because they want to make sure we are "for real".

Children will find strength in our modeling of appropriate coping skills or they will not. It is OK for them to be scared and it is OK for adults to be scared—it is how we portray our feelings and messages about the present and future that matter most. This is what most children are thinking about; right now and tomorrow. In order for them to continue to be socially, emotionally and academically successful (individually determined) they need reassurance about security and hope for now, later today, and tomorrow.

I attempt to teach teens the concept of developing coping skills through examples of relationships. I may say that even older people get hurt and cry over failed relationships, but most cope appropriately with such an event. In other words, it is unlikely to see a single fifty-year old male teacher punching a locker when his lady friend breaks up with him. So the idea of learning how to cope becomes a real possibility and it instills hope when we can get this message across.

Schools can be incredible institutions. They all have the potential to help prepare **our** children for their individual futures through academic and social guidance. The exceptional schools do not ignore the emotional well-being of children. Whatever challenges such schools face, whether it has to do with acts of terrorism or tragedies within the school district's family, these schools will do right. These exceptional schools will not ignore the emotional well-being of their children and staff because they recognize its impact upon the educational processes of the children.

My basic premise and message when attempting to help children through such challenges is this: I remind children of some challenges this country has experienced. I may say it has not always been easy, but we typically overcome them, or that the hope and belief we will overcome them, remains strong. I would like to say that the peoples of many other nations in this world do not have a strong sense of this "hope and belief". Hope and belief in a safer nation and world is not a given. Politicians may want to step in here and argue, but at these moments my motives are not to engage or espouse in any political agenda. The motives are to help children. My language in such conversations with children alters depending upon their age and maturity level. Young children do not need specific details. I may tell young children that the adults will continue to protect them and that I want them to continue to play with their friends and learn at school, etc.

I may talk to older children about sacrifices and hard decisions that have to be made for the world to be a safer place for them. Again, I responsibly stay away from political agendas in such discussions. I may talk about consequences, but that the likely outcome will be a better world. I then tell older children to continue to play, learn and plan for their futures (proms, career interests, college, etc.). I realize many adults do not know what to say or how to say it, but my message will always end with a sense of security and hope. I believe this is the key to such dialogues with children—that the message ends with a sense of security and hope.

Adults do not have to explain their concerns about terrorism and loss in detail whenever a child asks a question about such issues. You will place an incredible amount of pressure on yourself if you feel you must come up with a great answer or response. In fact, you may not have an understanding of these issues, you may become emotional when you discuss these topics, or you may have the tendency to go to a political place. Trust me; your response under these circumstances may not help the child. It may help you to get something off your chest, show off your political savvy (or not), but try to remember this is not about you. You are not alone in this struggle.

During emotional times, I believe it is sometimes OK to share tears, frustration, and anger with children, it is the manner and message you give while doing so that is crucial for the well-being of the child. Remember, the instillation of security and hope. I try to stick to a bottom line — terrorist acts are evil and losing friends and family members are tragic losses, but we will move forward, we will get through this together, and we will try to become stronger. If you are uncomfortable discussing these topics with children or have the propensity for gloom and doom scenarios I ask you to consider the following: Strengthen your own support systems and cease surrounding yourself with other gloomers and doomers. Some responses you may offer are as follows: I don't have an answer or response for you right now, but I know someone that may, or,

I am really upset at the moment about this and I am seeking some guidance also. When adults are ingenuous, children feel it—they may not hear it in your well manicured words, but they will feel it. What you will have accomplished is the development of mistrust and uncertainty. I do not believe you want this to be your teaching.

Being honest with yourself and with children is not a cop-out, it is truth. There should be no shame in truth. The most important lesson you can teach when not able to address these issues with children is the lesson of truth. It cannot stop there, however. You must express concern by making sure the child moves toward an adult that can assist them and then follow-up with them later to show your genuine concern. And maybe down the road when you have processed the situation/information you can revisit the issue with the child when appropriate.

During times of crisis, regardless of what the crisis may be, I suggest the following strategies or ideas to be considered:

—It will not help you and certainly not your children to watch the news extensively, especially before bedtime. There is something to be said for sitcoms or really simple funny TV/movies.

—You may want to consider engaging your family in different activities together. When was the last time you all participated in making a meal together, playing a board game together, etc?

—When was the last time you got in touch with an old

friend? Pick one that was uplifting and catch up on events with him or her.

—Whatever your faith, consider practicing it more. If faith is not a part of your belief system consider strengthening your more earthly strategies to deal with such events.

—Be careful not to frequently put yourself in the company of somber, gloom and doom personalities. If this is not possible, attempt to counter this with an increase in time spent around personalities that exhibit more positive energy and humor.

—Remember, stress, grieving and fear will challenge the productivity of your immune system. Increase your attention to a healthy diet that includes consistent intake of fruits and vegetables. It is quite simple to cut such foods up and have them around as snacks when those suffering are not eating full meals. I encourage this in school settings as well.

—Give instrumental music a chance. For example, take some time to listen to some classical music or new age piano.

—Remember, alcohol in excess can negatively affect your immune system. It can become a depressant and also interfere with your sleep patterns.

—Explore your interests in old hobbies or consider exploring involvement in new hobbies.

—Consider human service volunteer work. Meeting the needs of others often has a significant positive impact on the emotional well-being of the giver. Explore what is out there in the world of volunteering.

—Increase your physical activity. This has long been recognized as a good strategy to reduce stress.

—Allow an increase of appropriate humor into your life. This is another tried and proven method to decrease stress in life.

—Address sleeping and eating problems with your family physician, school nurse, and/or pediatrician. Sleeping and diet are essential to healing.

These are difficult times and we are being challenged to meet needs of children not previously considered or experienced. The school system and school personnel are accountable for their students for approximately seven hours a day for approximately 13 years. Most can acknowledge we should not be forcing a specific religious belief on children in public schools, nor be enlisting dramatic child rearing concepts that go against basic parenting philosophies. That being said, world tragedies and conflicts do prompt a need for a sense of security in the eyes of children. Silent prayer and the Pledge of Allegiance for example, have been mechanisms which historically promoted such security. In our Country, we do not tell children who to pray to, what to pray for, or that they must pray – just allow for the silence for others and the Pledge of Allegiance speaks to the citizenship argument presented earlier. Citizenship unites, and with unity comes strength and security. As for discipline, the concept of logical consequences is perhaps the most transparent and simplest form of discipline one can implement.

In considering all of these factors, we are addressing teamwork through consistency, compassion, and messages of security and hope for a better today and tomorrow.

We are all challenged to watch what messages we give to our children because of the political nature of our country and world. Please let us not be like those on the far right and far left positions of the political continuum that are so consumed with their own belief system that no other opinions matter. We simply cannot teach effectively with anger and disingenuous motives in our hearts and words, unless of course, we are trying to teach anger and dishonesty. If this is the case, we will teach quite effectively. Look at the state of affairs in countries that have accepted such teaching; how they behave toward those who think, live and practice religion differently. Many of their children know no other world but one consumed by hate.

I worry about the damage the behavior of our own political system is doing to our children. This damage will inevitably visit all of us as these children grow-up to become angry, hateful, and/or rigid thinkers. We have much control when people on the political continuum (liberals, independents and conservatives) behave in such manners — shun them, don't defend them, don't vote for them. Don't continue to accept such behavior simply because they reside somewhere within your political party. Shameful, hateful and dishonest arguments against each other model terrible messages to children. Be responsible in your viewpoints; be respectful of other's viewpoints, and with integrity and dignity, attempt to make the world a better place for our children. Contrary to what many political leaders seem to believe, passion for what one believes does not have to involve the negative behaviors often expressed. The leader who maintains integrity and dignity when confronted by irrationality and negativity will win in the bigger picture. Thus, the ultimate victory — He or she has taught other leaders, masses of people from far away places, peers, elders and most importantly, children, well.

Perhaps a different mechanism to monitor our schools for the behaviors mentioned prior would be well-developed Parent-Teacher Associations and should students be involved, even better. If training were offered regarding fair/balanced/appropriate discussions of politics, immigration, religious expression, and school wide discipline issues, this may be a real possibility. After all, our parents and teachers typically have the most impact on the lives of children in our schools. This could only work if the Associations were to be lead, managed and trained with integrity. If others want to have a voice in such monitoring, join your PTA. Just an idea, what do you think?

SECTION IV

SCHOOL LEADERSHIP—A MESSAGE AND PLEDGE
Administrators, Superintendents and Board members

Your Pledge:

I understand my role is crucial in helping parents, teachers and all school personnel care for and educate all of our children. Appropriate training and support for paraprofessionals, transportation, cafeteria, maintenance and clerical personnel must be recognized within this objective. In matters of money, hiring, firing and other areas of decision making, my motives will always be in the best interests of our children. I will not allow personal issues or negative aspects of politics to interfere in this cause. I will uphold integrity and accountability regarding decisions to change placements, suspend, or expel children by exploring the interventions prior. I understand this exploration may not change an individual outcome, yet it will maintain and/or increase accountability standards for future decisions. I understand meeting the needs of children with special needs should not be compared to what is good for the masses. I understand educating all of our children is not always an equal process, but a matter of fairness in providing an appropriate education for every child.

Signature:_____

Date:_____

Folks, if you struggled with signing this pledge, please explore the resistance with some trusted friends or co-professionals. The signing of the pledge is for your conscience only.

_____

_____

_____

_____

_____

_____

_____

_____

_____

_____

_____

_____

_____

SECTION V

IN CLOSING

*Parents/Caregivers: Become active in your school's Parent-Teacher Association!

*Teachers/Paraprofessionals: Become active in your school's Parent-Teacher Association!

*School and District Leadership, Service Providers and all other School Personnel: Become active in your schools' and district's Parent-Teacher Associations!

Can I be a better teacher, paraprofessional, parent/ caregiver, leader, professional or support staff?

If yes, what am I willing to do to increase my skills?

_____

_____

_____

_____

_____

_____

DAVID M. WILLSON

WELCOME

TO

THE

GOOD FIGHT!